To Paul Giblen,

God bless your mission

Sincerely,
Dan Montgomery

God and Your Personality

God and Your Personality

by

Dr. Dan Montgomery

With a preface by John Powell, SJ

Pauline
ST. PAUL BOOKS & MEDIA
BOSTON

Library of Congress Cataloging in Publication Data

Montgomery, Dan, 1946–
  God and your personality / by Dan Montgomery.
    p. cm.
  Includes bibliographical references and index.
  ISBN 0-8198-3075-5 (pbk.)
  1. Personality—Religious aspects—Christianity. 2. Spiritual life—Catholic Church. 3. Catholic Church—Doctrine. I. Title.
  BV4597.58.M66 1995
  248.4—dc20   95-3256
                                                                            CIP

Cover Photo credit: Mary Emmanuel Alves, FSP

The Scripture quotations contained herein are from the *Revised Standard Version Bible with the Apocrypha/Deuterocanonical Books*, copyrighted © 1973 by the Division of Christian Education of the National Council of Churches of Christ in the U.S.A., and are used by permission. All rights reserved.

Some material in chapters one and twelve originally appeared in *Guideposts* magazine.

Copyright © 1995 by Dan Montgomery

Printed and published in the U.S.A. by Pauline Books & Media, 50 St. Paul's Avenue, Boston, MA 02130.

Pauline Books & Media is the publishing house of the Daughters of St. Paul, an international congregation of women religious serving the Church with the communications media.

1 2 3 4 5   99 98 97 96 95

*To Katie,
my beloved wife and editor,
who stands with me in every way.
And to
The Daughters of St. Paul,
for inviting me to write this book.*

About the Author

Dr. Dan Montgomery is a licensed clinical psychologist with 25,000 hours of counseling experience. In addition to his work in private practice, he has taught in four universities, holding advanced degrees in psychology and philosophy. An internationally known conference speaker, his magazine articles are read by 30 million people worldwide. Dr. Montgomery may be contacted by writing c/o:

Pauline Books & Media
50 St. Paul's Avenue
Boston, MA 02130

Table of Contents

Preface	x
1. God and Your Personality	12
2. Compass of the Self	20
3. The Core of Personality	34
4. The Dependent Christian	42
5. The Aggressive Christian	54
6. The Withdrawn Christian	66
7. The Controlling Christian	78
8. Beyond Manipulation	95
9. Techniques for Transformation	104
10. Befriending Your Unconscious	119
11. Images of God	134
12. The Prayer Compass	144
13. Change in Your Own Backyard	162
A Word to the Reader	167
How to Start a "God and Your Personality" Book Study	168
Notes	170
Index	174

Preface

It always puzzled me that Jesus was unable to do his works of power where there was no faith. I reasoned (to myself) that if he had done his works of power where there was no faith, faith might have been stirred in some of his hearers.

Then one day a woman who taught with my Mother was miraculously cured of a terminal disease. When she asked her doctor to testify to the miracle of her cure he said: "Helen, I've tried to keep this from you as long as possible. But now I must tell you: I do not believe in God. I will testify that on this date you had terminal cancer and today you are completely healthy. But I'm not going to postulate a God to explain what I do not understand."

When the lady told me of this, for the first time I understood that it takes faith to accept and interpret the power of God and his deeds.

Like physical medicine, psychology as such is a natural science. It deals only with the mind and body of humans. A psychologist as such does not recognize divine power or intervention. However, if the psychologist is also a believer he looks at the reality of the human person through the eyes of science and faith.

The author of these pages, Dr. Dan Montgomery, is one of these. He is a student of human nature but he looks at humans in need of healing through the eyes of science and of faith. He combines his knowledge of psychology with that knowledge of humans that can come only from the relationship with God.

As I read through these pages, I wondered if this integration of the natural with the supernatural isn't what is needed today. I myself feel "stationed" by God at this position. It was good to know that there are others, like the author of this book, who are stationed there too.

The book itself is very readable. It says things with clarity and simplicity. Still, it is not superficial. An old adage pertains to the wisdom of these pages—"This will work if you work at it." I would strongly recommend to readers that they do the exercises included, and that they test the wisdom in this book through discussion.

Those who have worked with the Scriptures are familiar with the terms literary *genre* or literary type. If a piece is a work of poetry, you cannot apply the norms used, for example, in the interpretation of history. In the interpretation of Scripture, it is very important to recognize the literary type before attempting to explain the contents.

Is our author writing "psychology" or "theology?" I would suggest that this literary type raises the natural science to the level of faith, and that faith is used to understand the natural. At least I felt as though I were reading the word of God as it is imprinted on the minds and hearts of us humans.

John Powell, SJ
Loyola University
Chicago
1994

One

God and Your Personality

JESUS CHRIST WAS THE SON OF GOD and a marvelously healthy human being. During his earthly life he radiated the power and benefits of a balanced personality. He was true to himself and at the same time revealed the personality of the Father, saying, "He who has seen me has seen the Father" (Jn 14:9). His attitudes, emotions and actions showed us what it means to have God at work in our personalities.

The impact of Christ's personality on others was contagious, leading to surprising transformations. John, the son of thunder, became the beloved disciple. The impulsive Peter changed into Cephas, the rock. Mary Magdelene, the harlot, became a serene woman filled with dignity and faith. All who faithfully followed the Lord found the loving promptings of his Spirit at work within them.

How can we participate more fully in the transformation of our lives and personalities? This book shows how God is at work in us today, prompting us toward health, balance and creativity. Jesus still transforms those who follow him. I know. My personality has needed regular tune-ups over several decades, but required a major overhaul when I met the Lord at the age of seventeen.

Las Vegas, New Mexico, was a dangerous place when I was growing up in the late 1950's. Maybe it was a throwback to our wild west past. One year we had twenty-one murders, several right across from the local movie theater. That's a lot of killing for a town of 14,000.

Once I saw a man walking down Grand Avenue carrying a deer rifle. He whirled and aimed at me. Before I could react he turned the gun on himself and pulled the trigger. I never felt safe as a kid in Las Vegas. I was always afraid.

I started off as a gentle, curious boy. I collected stamps, flew kites and raised horned toads. I kept an old box turtle named Quonk Quonk. But in the sixth grade, my life changed. I was sledding one afternoon when a gang of boys attacked me. Jimmy, the leader, beat me until I lay unconscious in the snow. Two friends dragged me home. Years later Jimmy went to the state hospital for murdering his father.

In Junior High School I spent a lot of time trying to avoid getting beat up. My best friend, Lewis, lived across the alley. Lewis was smart and fun. We studied together, went to school together and tried to protect each other. He was the only person I laughed around. But despite the friendship, a seething chemistry of dark emotions brewed within me.

At fifteen I was beaten for the last time. A couple of gang members jumped me at lunch and knocked me out with brass knuckles. The next week I found the toughest boy in school. His older brothers were golden gloves boxing champs. He had a rattlesnake tattoo on one arm and a switchblade plunged into a heart on the other. I asked him to teach me to fight.

We met for ten brutal sessions in the gym. The final time something inside me snapped, like a taut rubber band. *I'm not going to take this anymore, not from anyone.* I exploded with a vicious right fist that knocked him cold. As he went down I felt the heady surge of brute power and vengeance.

Within a week I chased down one of the guys who'd jumped me at lunch and punched him out. The next day three of his buddies cornered me in an alley. I beat the leader to a pulp. The others ran. Suddenly I wanted to fight anyone who looked at me crosswise. When my Latin teacher threatened to send me to the principal's office for acting up in class, I promised to destroy his car if he did. He backed down and I felt powerful. I no longer wanted to just protect myself; I wanted to prove myself.

One night when I was sixteen I invited a group of kids to my house for a party. Lewis and I made punch and sandwiches. I danced to *Blue Suede Shoes* with Marcia, my girlfriend. Then some uninvited older boys came in. One was Monty, a neighbor and the center on our football team.

I told Monty and his friends to get lost. Monty looked at me, surprised. That look was all it took. I decked him and then followed up with a flurry of blows while he lay helpless on the floor. It took three boys to pull me off. Lewis and Marcia looked on in horror as Monty's friends carried him to their car.

If I don't stick up for myself, who will? I rationalized. Yet deep inside I was shaken. Monty hadn't done anything to deserve that vicious attack.

I started drinking on the weekends. That was like dousing a fire with gasoline. One Saturday night I was returning from a hunting trip with some friends. We came up on a motorcycle with two riders—Carlos and Julio, a couple of toughs who'd beaten me up in junior high. I shouted to Bobby, who was driving, "Pull up next to them!" Then I thrust my shotgun out the window just a few feet from Julio's head. He looked at me in horrified recognition. I was glad he knew why I was pointing that gun at him. I pulled back the hammer and put him in my sights. Then I raised the barrel about three inches above Julio's head before pulling the trigger. The blast sent them flying off the road and spinning into a ditch where they cursed us as we roared off.

I was out of control. My parents were called into the principal's office to hear about my drinking. All my friends deserted me, except for Lewis. Then one night I turned on him. We argued at a party. Lewis left in a car with some friends. I went berserk with fear, betrayal and rage. I jumped in my car in hot pursuit, the speedometer breaking a hundred. I caught up with them on Seventh Street and cut them off at a stop sign. Adrenaline poured through my body as I jumped out of my car and sped around to the passenger side, where Lewis was sitting. He didn't have time to roll up the window. I pummeled him. Some of my blows landed wildly on the steel frame of the window, shredding my knuckles. Yet I felt no pain, only rage. To this day I can still recall the look of confused fear on Lewis's face as I hit him again and again.

I'd lost my best friend, and could only blame myself. I felt terrible. *You've got to control your temper,* I told myself. *You're turning into a maniac.* I resolved to straighten up. I could control this thing. For a while life went smoothly. Then, in the fall of my senior year, Marcia broke up with me and started dating Mike, the new guy in town. I wanted to kill him.

Mike threw a huge party at the Castanada Hotel ballroom. Everyone was invited—except me. I got good and drunk, then drove my '57 Chevy over to the party. I made my way to the door and demanded to go in. When the chaperones asked to see my invitation, I went crazy. I screamed at Mike over the arms and bodies of parents who were desperately trying to restrain me, "Come out and fight like a man!" Buddy Holly's *Peggy Sue* was playing in the background. All the kids stopped dancing and peered at me. Vodka and the urge for revenge made me feel like I could fight them all. Only when one of the parents started to phone the police did I back off. Still in a blind fury, I jumped in my car and peeled out, tires screaming, radio blaring.

Deep in my heart I hated what I'd become. Where was that sensitive child I'd once been? Now I never laughed or smiled. I wore a poker face and a mean stare to keep people away. I was digging a deeper and deeper hole for myself, and there seemed to be no way out.

Four nights after threatening Mike at the party, I was walking home with a half pint of vodka stuffed in my old leather jacket. The autumn coolness chilled my face. I passed an old church on the corner of University and Eighth Street. As I stood at the stoplight, singing reached my ears. I didn't like churches. I hated organ music. But a strange feeling grew in my heart—a friendly energy coming from the church, beckoning me through the big oak double doors.

Suddenly I was aware of a desperate emptiness inside, and a longing so deep I had no words for it. It consumed me. I wanted the peace God could bring.

The stoplight changed to green. I didn't move. The music faded. *What will people say if I go in?* I started to cross the street, but the tug on my heart strengthened. Suddenly I turned back and walked up the steps to those big double doors, pulled one open and went inside.

It was a Wednesday evening service. Heads turned as I walked in and I knew people recognized me. My face heated up and I sat down quickly in the nearest seat. They'll probably throw me out, I figured. But instead, the friendliness that had touched me at the stoplight felt more personal, like a presence.

The reverend was talking about Christ. He said that Jesus could enter a person's life through the heart and bring peace to every corner of that life. Suddenly I was aware of a desperate emptiness inside, and a longing so deep I had no words for it. It consumed me. I wanted the peace God could bring. I knew that without it I would die.

God and Your Personality / 17

After the service I went to the communion rail. I asked Christ to enter my violent heart and bring peace. *I give my life to you,* I prayed. When I stood up the warmth of His love flooded me and tears streamed down my cheeks. Where emptiness had been minutes before, an indescribable peace filled my very being. For the first time in as long as I could remember, I wasn't afraid.

On the way to school the next morning I spotted Mike walking alone on the other side of the street. As I ran over to him he threw down his books and squared off. "Are you going to bust me up, Montgomery?" he shouted.

"Mike," I said, stopping in front of him. "I want to apologize for acting like a jerk at your party." I thrust out my hand. Mike eyed me suspiciously.

"Is this a trick?" he demanded.

"No," I answered. "Something incredible happened last night. I still don't completely understand it. But I don't want to fight. I want to be friends."

Mike searched my eyes, then took my hand. "All right, Danny. I believe you."

That handshake was a beginning. I spent a lot of time that school year making amends to all the people I had hurt. It was hard. But the peace that had come into my heart, and my involvement in the church spurred me on.

Over the next several years I experienced the most fascinating of paradoxes. God transformed my violence, suspicion and anger into empathy, trust and love. Then he called me to become a clinical psychologist. I've served him in the ministry of counseling and psychotherapy for almost twenty-five years. I've seen firsthand how knowledge of one's personality can open new doors of intimacy with God and one's fellows.

Priest-psychologist lgnace Lepp wrote: "Every individual has a moral obligation to tend toward maximum self-development.... The mystics, in claiming that God is to be discovered in the self, are well aware of what they are saying. It is by neglecting self that so many have become really incapable of finding God."[1] When people neglect self-development, they suffer symptoms of that neglect. This book is written for anyone who:

- faces the question: "Who am I?"
- feels anxiety about relationships
- experiences bouts of depression
- is trapped by shyness
- has a history of hostile outbursts
- feels apathy about their spiritual life
- often feels guilty
- is overly compulsive
- needs to recover from a painful past
- needs everyone's approval
- has trouble making decisions
- has a difficult family life
- wants a closer walk with God

The two main thrusts of this book include: 1) how to experience personality transformation using powerful psychological principles; and 2) how to deepen your friendship and appreciation of Jesus Christ. A new tool for developing both a healthy balance of personality and a vibrant spirituality is the *Compass of the Self,* presented in chapter two.

By prayerfully applying this personality compass, you'll understand yourself and others as never before. You'll see how to liberate your personality from past wounds or current rigidities. You'll outgrow patterns of dependency, aggression, withdrawal or control. Your awareness of the Holy Spirit in your daily life will deepen.

EXERCISES

1. Reflect back on a time when you needed God. What were the circumstances? Are you continuing to build on the relationship with him that you began at that time? Relationships require continued desire, openness and commitment. I suggest you spend a few concentrated moments today or tonight reestablishing your openness and desire for God.

2. If your connection to God has been diminished by doubt, worry, fear, unanswered prayer, guilt, procrastination, or anything else, then I suggest that you give the Holy Spirit permission to fill you anyway. Write down on paper all the reasons you don't feel close to God. Now tear the paper to shreds and throw it into a waste basket. Nothing can separate you from the Father's incredible love as expressed through his Son, Jesus Christ.

3. To gain valuable insight into yourself and others, write down in a prayer diary what perplexes, hurts or frustrates you most about yourself or others. After each entry, pray for Christ to assist you to develop new wisdom for coping. Read back through your prayer diary each week to discover the answers to your needs.

4. I suggest that you mark this book with highlights and margin notes. The greatest university in the world is your own private library. Master the material. Ask the Holy Spirit to help you digest it. Mark relevant sections for re-reading months or even years from now.

Two

Compass of the Self

JESUS' MESSAGE CHALLENGES EVERY MAN, woman and child to participate in the most profound of all revolutions—the transformation of his or her own personality. Jesus was concerned more than anything else with the quality of human life, including the relationships between men and women and the prizing of little children. He knew that healthy personalities strengthen family life and enable people to do God's will. He emphasized that the power of the Holy Spirit and the courage to love can help us live creatively.

While the Pharisees placed all their emphasis in religious life on external actions regulated by rules, Jesus believed it was possible to keep all the rules and not please God. He was more concerned with what a person becomes than with what he or she does. Not that he believed actions to be insignificant. But Jesus knew that our inner attitudes determine our outer behaviors. For Christ, the secret of pleasing God is to be found in *the spontaneous activities of a transformed personality:* "A sound tree cannot bear evil fruit, nor can a bad tree bear good fruit" (Mt 7:18).

The message of Jesus exploded the old wineskins of self-righteous religion and poured out the new wine of the Holy Spirit. The

Holy Spirit is central to a healthy personality, because the Holy Spirit flows like a wellspring through our inner cores, filling our lives with surprise and adventure. I'll speak more about the Holy Spirit in the next chapter, "The Core of Personality." But here I want to focus on how Jesus' personality—and how we can emulate him—provides the key to developing our capacity for healthy identity, intimacy and loving community.

As a psychologist, I am fascinated by Jesus' personality. Christ's personality was not rigid or one-sided, but revealed a dynamic rhythm of self-expression. He was *loving* enough to free and restore a woman caught in the act of adultery when her accusers wanted to stone her to death. This shows Christ's mercy. He was *assertive* enough to make a whip and physically drive the money changers from the temple. This shows Christ's righteous indignation. He was *weak* enough to surrender to being put to death on a cross and buried in another man's tomb. This shows Christ's humility. He was *strong* enough to do the Father's will, and to rise from the grave a victor over death itself. This shows Christ's lordship over all things in heaven and on earth.

Jesus exhibited the free-swinging polarities of a healthy personality. He was variously called the Rose of Sharon (love), the Lion of Judah (assertion), the Lamb of God (weakness), and the Prince of Peace (strength). *In Christ, we see God's design for a balanced personality.*

Compass of the Self

We need these Christ-like compass points to understand our personalities today. Let me explain what I mean by the term balanced personality. The personality compass can be compared to a physical compass used to determine direction: north, south, east or west. The two sets of polar opposites are located on the perimeter of a circle. North is the opposite of south; east is the opposite of west.

Particularly when low-hanging clouds obscure the sun by day and the stars by night, a compass can show us the way to go—as long as it works properly. As long as the needle is able to swing freely and rhythmically in all four directions, we know how to find our way home.

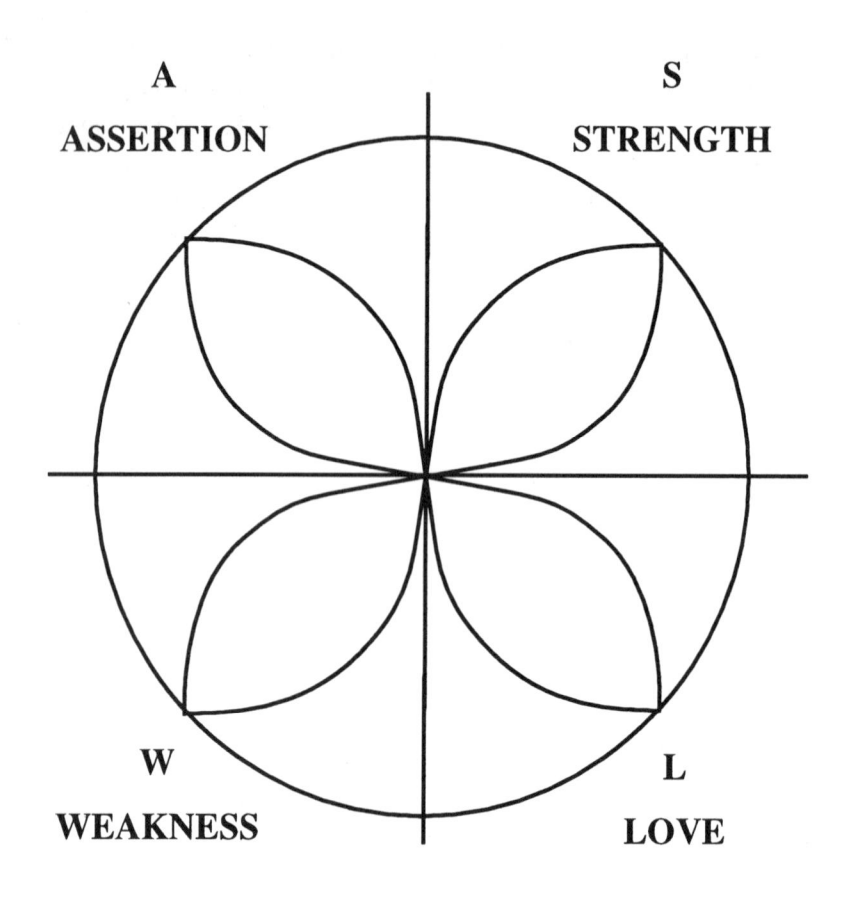

A
ASSERTION

S
STRENGTH

W
WEAKNESS

L
LOVE

COMPASS OF THE SELF

If the self is symbolized as a circle, then we can picture two personality polarities crisscrossing at the center of a person's compass. The four reference points around the perimeter act as inner guides. These four poles can be called *Love, Assertion, Weakness* and *Strength*. You can remember these compass points by using the acronym *LAWS*.

The compass points of love and assertion speak to the fundamental ways we feel about others; the weakness and strength poles represent a continuum of how we feel about *ourselves*. Catholic pastoral theologian Henri Nouwen emphasizes that to live a spiritual life "means first of all to come to the awareness of the inner polarities between which we are held in tension."[2] Understanding and monitoring these key polarities brings us into personality balance.

The Love Pole

Love is more than a feeling; it is a commitment to the highest good for others and ourselves. This is how God relates to humanity and how he inspires us to relate to each other. When the love pole is intact, we experience emotions of warmth, tenderness, caring and joy.

But many people throw love out of their emotional repertoire because they don't want to be vulnerable. They lose trust in themselves and others. They become defensive and cover their hearts with an iron breastplate. Those who are unwilling to remove this protective shield find themselves trapped behind a partial perspective that blocks wholeness.

Love plays a major role in enabling us to reach out for comfort, friendship and understanding. Love brings excitement and freshness to life. We feel like we *belong* when love is flowing—that we can express our fears, needs and dreams. Healthy love is a two-way street, letting us heal the wounds in others while we ourselves are being healed. Love involves feeling emotionally and spiritually connected to others. Love is the lifeblood of the Christian life and a healing balm in a broken world. Jesus said, "By this all men will know that you are my disciples, if you have love for one another" (Jn 13:35).

No one can be truly healthy without an outgoing spirit of love in their personality. But wrongly used, love can be a terrible trap. Love is never a license for another person to walk all over us. Masochism is a distortion of love which means that we think so little of ourselves that others can abuse us. We are in such dire need of approval that we surrender our dignity to get it.

Masochistic love sacrifices our health and well-being—supposedly to make someone else happy. Chapter four on "The Dependent Christian" will deal with this. Healthy love doesn't allow others to use or abuse us.

In marriage or friendship, healthy love brings affection, tolerance and prizing the other person. It enables us to forgive the other and accept ourselves. Growing in love means learning to say, "I am accepting," "I am supportive," "I am nurturing," and "I can express tender caring." The *virtue of caring* arises from the love pole.

Healthy love requires the balance of assertion, strength and weakness. When we love in wholesome ways we relate to others through balanced *interdependence*—not too independent or too dependent—and communicate without a need to control or be controlled. Healthy love empowers us to fulfill the great commandment which Jesus gave us: "And he said to him, 'You shall love the Lord your God with all your heart, and with all your soul, and with all your mind. This is the great and first commandment. And a second is like it, You shall love your neighbor as yourself'" (Mt 22:37-39).

The Assertion Pole

The opposite pole from love, and an equally important emotion, is assertion or anger. Assertion helps us stand up for ourselves without undue anxiety, to express ourselves comfortably, to negotiate for the things we need, to exercise our reasonable rights without denying the rights of others, and to say no without feeling guilty.

Assertion applies to the most ordinary of circumstances. For instance, do we honestly and openly express our feelings and values—even in the face of disagreement? Assertion helps us face the more difficult moments of life without cowering, enabling us to persevere even in tribulation. For example, we may need to confront a person over an injustice or challenge an evil situation.

Assertion provides the rocket fuel to blast out of circumstances that threaten to entrap or damage us. Assertion brings the tenacity required to follow God's will.

I find it unfortunate that the assertion pole is so often associated with telling people off, "flipping someone the bird," getting violent or demanding our way. Being obnoxious or aggressive are distortions of assertion that arise when we are out of balance with love.

Actually, the test of maturity on the assertion pole is whether we can assert ourselves without being hateful, spiteful or unforgiving. Maturity means that we take a stand without burning bridges, that we express ourselves while listening to others. In healthy assertion we may feel angry or resentful, but we seek a diplomatic channel of communication instead of just lashing out.

Appropriate assertion serves the ends of love and justice in the world. It empowers us to fight against unfairness, exploitation and phoniness. Jesus did this with the moneychangers in the temple and with the self-righteous Pharisees. Growth in the assertion polarity means saying, "I am expressive," "I can challenge," "I can confront," and "I can make a difference." Just as compassion flows from the love pole, the *virtue of courage* arises from a healthy use of the assertion pole.

The Weakness Pole

The weakness pole is too often scorned in today's culture, even by Christians. Often people (especially men) are taught to grin and bear it, never fail, beat the competition and never show neediness or tears. Such an attitude is most unfortunate. It keeps many people from becoming truly humble.

But weakness doesn't mean feeling low self-esteem or constantly failing in our endeavors. It means accepting the vulnerabilities that come with life. No one is king of the mountain forever. We need to accept occasional weakness without magnifying it. We need to face our limitations so we can improve them. Weakness is the royal road to reliance on God. We call upon God and he can save us. By acknowledging our shortcomings we are strengthened.

---

*Life can become bleak for a season.
But if we confess our needs to God and friends,
then setbacks which stun us
are often transformed into victories
of growth and recovery.*

Seasons of weakness are blessed times for soul-searching. They remind us not to be superior, self-contained or arrogant. We remember that apart from God's will, our lives shrink into nothingness. Weakness forms the spiritual tension of personality, the fact that we can affirm meaning even in the midst of evil, pain and mortality. Life can become bleak for a season. But if we confess our needs to God and friends, then setbacks which stun us are often transformed into victories of growth and recovery. "[We] won strength out of weakness" (Heb 11:34).

Another aspect of the weakness pole is accepting anxiety as a normal part of human existence. Many people seek to avoid anxiety at all costs. This is an irrational goal in life. We need to learn how to handle anxiety, not evade it. We all feel uncertain, anxious and helpless at times.

When we feel weak, we don't have to panic. We can relax and surrender to weakness, reminding ourselves that it is essential to a balanced personality. By being patient, we find that weakness eventually swings back into strength and courage. Reinhold Niebuhr's prayer says this well: "God, grant me the serenity to accept the things I cannot change, the courage to change the things I can, and the wisdom to know the difference."

A healthy acceptance of weakness means sometimes saying, "I am imperfect," "I feel vulnerable," "I need help," and "There is growth in the valley." The *virtue of humility* arises from the weakness compass point. However, we can only experience the healthy aspects of the weakness pole when all the other compass points are in balance.

The Strength Pole

Strength is a sense of adequacy and self-esteem. Reduced to its simplest level, strength is the inner affirmation that life is worth living. To feel good about our competencies is neither sinful nor selfish. Without self-esteem, we can esteem no one else. Without strength we can never make a contribution. Strength enables us to be original and creative, to bring into the world our unique gifts and talents.

American culture often encourages distortions of strength such as egoistic pride, self-righteousness, independence or blind ambition. Scripture warns us: "Pride goes before destruction" (Prov 16:18).

By contrast, healthy strength means doing what we can for ourselves, but asking for help when we need it. We admit when we're wrong, make amends quickly and show our caring openly.

Another attribute of healthy strength is using our power to benefit others, rather than lording it over them. Maturity on the strength polarity can be tested by such questions as these: Can I be competent without arrogance? Can I feel good about my strengths without judging others as less worthy than me? Can I make my own best efforts, yet ask for help when I need it? Do I use my confidence to cooperate with others, or to boss them around?

Human beings need to experience and express a sense of worth, confidence and dignity. We can follow many pathways to authentic strength, but the simplest one is by self-definition: I am a worthwhile human being. I don't need to act superior. I can be myself and accept other people as they are. Growth in the strength pole means saying, "I am adequate," "I am competent," "My life counts," and "I can contribute." The *virtue of esteem* arises from the strength pole.

Love isn't better than assertion, and strength isn't better than weakness. These four compass points simply reflect the potential God has created within us for becoming well-balanced, well-rounded people. These four basic poles of love and assertion, strength and weakness provide a latitude and longitude for psychological and spiritual well-being.

- *Love* is the glue which provides caring and tenderness in relationships

- *Assertion* enables us to stand up for ourselves and brings a sense of self-expression and courage

- *Strength* reflects our self-esteem, duty and power to contribute

- *Weakness* expresses that we are all imperfect and brings humility and empathy to our lives

If we ignore one or more of these compass points, we become stuck with a partial personality. Our personalities become rigid and one-sided. This inflexibility corrupts our perception of God. We foreclose our identity, diminish our capacity for intimacy and curtail our ability to participate in loving community. The Catholic philosopher Gabriel Marcel suggests an antidote to such an inauthentic existence in the "virtue of openness"[3]—openness to God, to our deepest selves and to personal growth.

Lack of personality balance shows up in four primary ways, depending upon where we are stuck in the balanced personality. Exaggerated love deteriorates into dependency. Out-of-control assertion escalates into aggression. Overblown weakness collapses into withdrawal. Inflated strength puffs up into compulsive control. Such patterns can trap us for years. We may pray for God's will to be done, yet resist his guidance through our rigid attitudes. I will explain these one-sided perspectives and show how to outgrow them in chapters four and seven.

The most common reason for being stuck in a partial personality style is that we were raised that way as children. Many women tilt too far toward the love pole because others labeled any expression of strength and assertion as too threatening, unlady-like or selfish. Many men are stuck on the assertion pole because their tender feelings were discouraged and they were taught to use anger to get their way. Individuals who were victimized as children often get stranded on the weakness pole, feeling hopeless and helpless. Others who were spoiled and praised too much grew up to be self-centered and perfectionistic. They are stuck on the strength pole.

Whether we call it sin or manipulation, *partial perspectives are exaggerated and rigid forms of functioning.* These disruptive patterns block the fluid spontaneity of healthy personality. They contaminate and interfere with healthy perceptions of self, others and God. They arrest personality development and block the spiritual transformation of personality. When we are prisoners to a partial personality, we grow no more. Fear, not love, becomes a pervading influence in our attitudes and behaviors.

To understand how fear works to constrict the core of a person, I use the analogy of the ameba, a tiny one-cell animal. If an ameba is repeatedly pricked by a pin, it permanently contracts itself to survive the attack. If a person is threatened psychologically or physically—especially early in life when basic personality is being formed—he or she learns to shrink back from psychological and spiritual awareness, to live defensively rather than wholeheartedly.

Self-defeating attitudes comprise partial personality styles. Such attitudes are false solutions wrongly applied. They are not our friends. The way out of each pattern is to take growth stretches into opposite compass points and gradually gain a balance of personality and relationships.

As the Holy Spirit guides us toward wholeness, love overcomes fear; assertion replaces helplessness; self-esteem ousts shame; and courage relieves self-doubt. We regain perspective and balance. *The Christ-like rhythm of love, assertion, weakness and strength can be restored.*

A Butterfly Experience

Elizabeth was a student of mine in a Catholic graduate school where I taught psychology. In her late thirties, having just added a third child to her family (and contemplating a fourth), she felt an inner urge to become a marriage and family counselor. My course helped her look at issues regarding raising a family, becoming a therapist and following her inner truth in Christ.

After a year of pursuing our program of studies, Elizabeth wrote the following:

> Whoever was the first to make the analogy between caterpillars and butterflies and death and resurrection—old life and new life—must have had a "butterfly experience." And to a certain degree, so have I.
>
> Knots being untied, tight jar lids being loosened—it is freedom. It is freeing. It is the slow motion experience of leaping through a meadow with arms and legs in tune with the rhythm of life. But somehow the butterfly says it best, because of the cocoon experience.
>
> People seem to have more than one go-round with the cocoon. How did it start for me this time? Why did it start?
>
> I was happy as a caterpillar. Just a bit confined, that's all. I viewed myself, and others did, as fuzzy-wuzzy, problem free,

happily married, financially secure, basking in the love of God...but I was not content.

I did not know myself. Actually, I did not even know that I did not know myself. And I certainly did not own my feelings. I had to move away from all those who unknowingly kept me as a pet caterpillar to learn the true situation. And that is why I ended up here at college.

Things have happened fast, which I like. But it has been a difficult, thrilling, laborious, joyous, arduous, climactic year. There have been so many significant encounters. Every week of classes I have learned so much. But several things were of major importance.

Almost a passing comment by Dr. Montgomery turned a trickle into a flood last fall when he said, "Liz, I sense a lot of tension in you—and have since we first met." I could hardly believe it. Everybody knew how calm, cool, and collected I always was. I was not tense...how could he say that?

I was only going to school full-time, keeping my husband happy, preparing three meals a day, cleaning the house, taking my son to Cub Scouts and piano lessons, taking my daughter to Brownies and ice skating, and giving constant attention to my new baby girl! Tense...tense! How true! I had to face it. *And so began a whole chain of discoveries.*

I thought I was relaxed and learned I was tense. I thought I was well-adjusted and learned that I did not even know myself. I thought I was loving and learned that I was often indifferent. I thought I was social and learned that I was withdrawn. On the positive side, I thought I was dumb and learned I was intelligent.

At an earlier point in my Christian life, it would have seemed unspiritual to consider these things. But somewhere near the beginning of this year, I experienced glorious assurance that God was in fact the one who had led me to this point—and he was leading me through!

For some reason, it seems that it is almost over. Or maybe it is the beginning of a new era of building on what I have learned. I do know that I am more excited about life. I love my husband and children more than ever before. I am more open to forming friendships with new people I meet. Most of all, I feel more comfortable being real with the Lord. In this year of growth I have come in touch with my own worth and potential.

Simply becoming aware was a great part of the answer. Perhaps that is because I wanted the change. I really do want to be a transparent person.

For now all I can say is that something deep is happening within me—and I love what is happening.

Personality transformation is a lifelong process. Sr. Bernadette Vetter speaks of this journey as "an opening of new doors, a becoming, a probing, a going inward to my center, a developing of relationships ... every arrival is a new beginning!"[4]

In the next chapter I will show how the Holy Spirit can flow like an artesian well through the center of our personalities and so transform us.

EXERCISES

1. Review your life to find times when you used each of these compass points in a healthy way. Describe in your prayer diary how the compass points provide a system of checks and balances within your personality. Ask God to strengthen any compass point that you presently ignore. Read each of these statements slowly and out loud. Can you make them your own?

- *Love:* "*I* can give support, nurturance, sympathy, and caring to others. I like and love myself. I believe in helping others and in trusting my instincts for self-preservation."

- *Assertion:* "*I* can express myself whether people approve or

not. I can say no to unreasonable or uncomfortable requests. I can stand up for what I need and express what I value."
- *Strength:* "*I* am adequate to the tasks of living. I can gain competence and confidence in new areas through practice, discipline, and mastery. I can feel pride for what I do well, and be willing to learn whatever will help me to succeed."
- *Weakness:* "*I* can relax about my occasional uncertainties and anxieties, knowing that these are part of the human condition. I can be aware of my limitations. I can ask for help when I need it. I can be humble and empathetic toward others when they are weak."

2. Do you find that one of these compass points is difficult for you to deal with? Talk over your discovery with a trusted friend. A missing or damaged compass point may be linked to a traumatic experience in your past. Pray about seeking a pastoral counselor or psychologist for assistance. Consider attending a healing and recovery workshop in your area.

Three

The Core of Personality

OUR SPIRITUAL CORE—THE CENTER OF our being—is the source of our God-given personhood and Christ's presence within. Jesus said, "Behold, the kingdom of God is within you" (Lk 17:21) (KJV). The Holy Spirit dwells within our core and inspires us to be witnesses to God's unfolding kingdom. The spiritual core reflects the fact that we are made in the image of God, and have an intimate relationship with him. We discover and actualize our identity in Christ by participating in the Body of Christ, including our local church.

Richard McBrien, Chairman of the Department of Theology, University of Notre Dame, writes: "This Kingdom, of course, is available to every human being as 'grace and mercy,' and yet each individual gains entrance through a total interior renewal which the Gospel calls *metanoia;* it is a radical conversion, a profound change of mind and heart. The Church itself comes into being as a community gathered in Jesus' name in order to seek together the Kingdom, build it up and live it.... It is a proclamation in word, in sacrament, in witness, and in service."[5]

Whether our potential for interior renewal is realized depends on how responsive we become to the Holy Spirit in our personalities. Who is the Holy Spirit, this mysterious third Person of the Trinity?

How can he become more to us, more than just a phrase recited in the Apostle's Creed? If we conceive of the Holy Spirit as an artesian well flowing through our innermost beings, he becomes more real to us.

What is an artesian well? The little New Mexico town of Artesia possesses some of these wells. An artesian well is made by boring deep into the earth until water is reached which then flows up by the force of internal pressure like a fountain. The originating source of the water is always higher up, from the top of a hill or mountain.

From this high point, the water seeps down underneath the earth and converges into a mighty stream. By drilling the well deep enough for its bottom to fall out, the core of the well connects to an underground reservoir of water. The force of nature pushes the water from the underground river up through the core of the well. An abundance of water becomes available at the surface of the artesian well. All that is required to keep the well flowing is for its core to stay clean and open.

Jesus said, "He who believes in me, as the scripture has said, 'Out of his heart shall flow rivers of living water.' Now this he said about the Spirit, which those who believed in him were to receive; for as yet the Spirit had not been given, because Jesus was not yet glorified" (Jn 7:38-39).

We need the life-force of the Holy Spirit to transform us into Christ-like personalities and to radically renew our interior being. However, receiving the flow of the Holy Spirit through our personalities may seem unfamiliar. We may need to understand more clearly how the Holy Spirit can infuse us with a deeper love for Jesus.

A Mighty Rushing Wind

Six years after my conversion, I still hungered to live closer to Jesus. My fears and doubts too often got the best of me. I wanted strength to be a more faithful follower. Intellectually, I knew about God's love, but I needed more tangible assurance to help me to grow in my friendship with him. At times God seemed so far away.

I studied the Bible in an effort to find direction. A host of scriptures spoke to me about the wisdom, power and love which the Holy Spirit imparts to those who belong to Jesus. I read about how he is the source of wisdom (Jn 14:26; 1 Cor 12:8), the source of miraculous power (Lk 24:49; Acts 1:8; Rom 15:19), the channel of God's love (Rom 5:3-5; Gal 5:22), and our Comforter in times of weakness (Rom 8:26). I needed this kind of companionship.

Now I had knowledge about the Holy Spirit. But I wanted to experience him firsthand and develop a relationship with him. I felt awkward and a little nervous, but decided it was time to ask God to introduce me to the Holy Spirit.

On a Friday night I slipped into an upstairs room in a church in my hometown. I'd been entrusted with the key because I often went there at night to pray. That night I came seeking an encounter with the Holy Spirit, but I didn't know exactly how to go about it.

I sat in the middle of a darkened room in a child's chair—the room was for little children. I bowed my head and pleaded, "Lord Jesus, I want to love you with all my heart. But too often I don't seem to know whether you're around or what you're doing. I need to feel your friendship so that I can tell others about you. The Bible says the Holy Spirit can help me, that he can fill me with love and power. So here I am. What happens next?"

For several minutes, silence enveloped the room. Finally, I decided that nothing was going to happen. I stood to leave when a sound like a mighty rushing wind roared down the hallway and burst into the room. A wave of electrifying power came into me. It filled me with incredible joy—and then fear! I shouted "Stop!" The wind stopped immediately.

Now, I'm a twentieth-century person raised in a culture based on science, analytical thinking and empirical proofs. At that time, I'd just received my Bachelor of Science degree. I felt incredulous at the sound and power of the wind, the Holy Spirit. It was okay to *read* about such a thing in the book of Acts, but mind-blowing to *experience* it here and now.

I walked to the window to see if the wind was blowing outside. The windows were shut tight. The summer night was still. The pounding of my heart reminded me that the sound of the rushing wind was real. I took a deep breath to calm myself. I decided to pray again and trust the experience no matter what.

"Okay, God," I said. "I'm ready now if you want to start the wind again." Suddenly the wind roared down the hall and into the room. It was terrifying and wonderful. Sweet sensations pulsed throughout my body. The wind and power became so strong that I again yelled "Stop!" All fell silent.

A tingling sensation developed around my heart and chest. Slowly, the pleasant sensations spread to my neck and jaw. My lips started quivering. I began stammering like a little child. I found myself starting to speak to God, but it was not in English. It was in another language which I have since come to call my "prayer language."

This strange new language didn't originate in my mind. It seemed to flow from my heart, from my deepest feelings. The emotional sense that accompanied my utterances was one of intimacy, of spontaneous and joyous communication. I prayed this way for an hour or so. Then the Holy Spirit lifted from me. I sat in silence practically glowing.

That was plenty for one night. I said, "Thank you, Jesus, for showing me your Spirit and your love! I'm sorry I got so scared. I just didn't know you did this kind of thing! Thank you for being so close to me. Help me to be your friend for life. Help me to love you and serve people until I meet you face to face."

From that night long ago until today, I continue to be fully human with all my foibles, flaws and blunders. But there is a loving power at work that binds my wounds and fans the fire of faith within me. The Holy Spirit kindles my own spirit and draws me into a more intimate relationship with God the Father and Jesus the Son.

Our Inner Spring of Grace

Priest-psychologist Adrian van Kaam writes: "We will see in eternal gratefulness how the inner spring of grace made our deepest self similar to Jesus. We will see how the spring inside us leaps up with dazzling splendor for all eternity."[6]

Trusting the Holy Spirit in our core means receiving God's power to become whole and rightly related to others. By coupling inspired self-understanding with God's grace, we can gradually give up worry, guilt and false pride. The Holy Spirit helps us develop *the courage to be our real selves in Christ.*

What I refer to as the *core,* Scripture refers to as the *heart.* In Scripture the word *heart* means the seat of life—your entire nature and understanding. Important aspects of the core self include:

- trust in your inner Supreme Court—your inner truth in Christ—for decision-making
- the ability to use your intelligence in open-minded and unprejudiced ways
- willingness to feel and express a full range of emotions including love and assertion, weakness and strength
- trust in your inner promptings, hunches and intuitions, knowing that these often correspond with God's will
- an openness in daily life to the mysterious ways that God works in your life and personality
- the courage to be a person-in-process, always growing in the art of living by the grace of God
- an inner attitude of prayer for the Holy Spirit to comfort and assist you

One of the paradoxes of personal growth is that we can never force it. We need to be patient with ourselves and others. Every person must grow at his or her own pace, in the wisdom of God.

Actively Pursuing Growth

By trusting the Holy Spirit in our cores, we surrender to the growth process for becoming Christ-like. As long as we remain open to this growth process, God imparts to us "the riches of his glory...[that]...you [may] be strengthened with might through his Spirit" (Eph 3:16). The Holy Spirit heals, inspires, comforts and guides us. He helps us face our unflattering traits and confess our shortcomings without feeling condemned. In being honest about our real selves, we grow more whole.

None of us lives from the core all the time, or perhaps even most of the time. Sin and self-will taint us all. Growth toward authentic personhood happens slowly. We cannot change ourselves suddenly even if we want to. Rather, real and enduring change is a gradual, steady process of becoming, like bulbs planted in a winter garden that eventually bloom in the springtime sunlight.

Inner growth is nurtured by the courageous acceptance of our whole being—strength and weakness, assertion and love. If we do not actively pursue growth, it may never happen, since God respects our free will. The opposite of actively pursuing growth is *resistance to growth*. Erroneous perspectives which resist personality growth include stubbornness, rigidity, hardness of heart and cynicism. The Holy Spirit encourages us to move from resistance to the joy of growing in grace. He helps us surrender, become more real, develop healthy love and celebrate daily life. All we need is the *courage to grow.*

The next four chapters describe how we can free ourselves from personality perspectives that hinder our spiritual growth: the dependent perspective; the aggressive perspective; the withdrawn perspective; and the controlling perspective. By facing and outgrowing these patterns, we can grow toward our Christ-like capacity for identity, intimacy and community.

RESISTANCE TO GROWTH	COURAGE TO GROW
STUBBORNNESS Doing the same thing again and again with no new learning. Beating our heads against a brick wall instead of looking for the corner. Being stiff-necked and proud. A partial personality style that overrides our potentials for identity, intimacy and community.	*SURRENDER* Listening to our spiritual intuitions and inner promptings. Discovering novel solutions to new problems, and creative solutions to old problems. Having a freshness of perception and a child-like openness to God. Flowing with the Holy Spirit instead of resisting him.
RIGID ROLES Being inflexible and fixed in our framework for living. Being repressed, judgmental and defensive. Living on automatic pilot. Plodding through life mechanically. Having tunnel vision. Hiding our hearts. Believing that our way is the only way. Striving to control ourselves, others and God.	*BEING REAL* Having an open mind, an expressive heart, a teachable spirit, and a responsive body. Being aware and expressive of love, assertion, weakness, and strength. Seeking to outgrow partiality and to develop a balanced personality. Relating wholeheartedly to Jesus and to people.
DISTORTIONS OF LOVE Manipulating ourselves and others through dependence, aggression, withdrawal, or control. Using every means to get love other than being our real selves. Believing that all is well without facing ourselves or relating intimately with others.	*HEALTHY LOVE* Expressing ourselves with sincerity and diplomacy. Learning to love people from inside their own skins. Using empathy and wisdom to sense people's hurts, hopes and needs. Practicing self-love, nurturance of others and love for Christ.
CYNICISM Being mounted like a dead butterfly instead of soaring like a live one. Psychospiritual rigor mortis. Feeding off feelings of fear, resentment, suspicion, and defensiveness. Living in self-will. Neglecting our inner depths and potentials. Missing the adventure of living.	*CELEBRATION OF LIFE* Experiencing the many miracles of life. Being intimate with God and seeking our heart's desires. Being of good cheer. Being healers, forgivers and givers of faith in God. Accepting our imperfections. Transforming culture. Seeking God for daily fellowship and guidance.

EXERCISES

1. Study the table on "Resistance to Growth" versus "Courage to Grow." Write in your prayer diary about any ways you've been stubborn, rigid, manipulative or cynical. Now sketch out ideas about how to be more growth-oriented, real, loving and positive. Write a prayer which tells God of your desire to grow and change.

2. Here is an exercise to deepen your capacity to relax, breathe in and sense God's peace. Find a quiet, private place—perhaps a favorite room at home. Pick a time of day with no distractions. Unplug the phone. Lie down on a sofa or on the floor. Get comfortable. Close your eyes and surrender the tensions in your body to the Holy Spirit.

Take several deep breaths from your belly, filling your abdomen like a balloon, then gently blow out all the air before inflating again. Allow tension and anxiety to drain out of you and the serenity of the Holy Spirit to flow through your core. Enjoy the sensations of warmth and heaviness, which tell you that your body is relaxing.

Identify any part of your body that remains tense. Deliberately tighten this area; then relax it. Scan your body from your forehead to the tips of your toes, offering your muscles, blood pressure and breathing to the Holy Spirit's care.

Meditate on the Bible verse, "Cast all your anxieties on him, for he cares about you" (1 Pt 5:7). Let go of your thoughts, worries and concerns. Allow your muscles to melt. Spend five or ten minutes savoring the reality that "underneath are the everlasting arms." Let the Holy Spirit breathe through you. Celebrate his comfort in your entire being.

Four

The Dependent Christian
(Love Compass Point)

NATALIE CAME INTO THERAPY because she was contemplating suicide. Her husband was worried about her and made the appointment. They had just been to San Francisco for a weekend. Natalie had become so depressed that her husband found her trying to open the window of their seventeenth floor hotel room. She wanted to jump out. I'm going to let Natalie tell her story.

> When I first came into therapy I had no idea what I felt inside myself. I was numb to my own feelings, except for a black depression. Even though I was functioning adequately at work, one of my sons said to me, "Mom, how come you don't smile or joke anymore?" I had worn a forced smile for years so that everything would go smoothly and I wouldn't have to deal with conflict. My chief role was to make everyone around me happy.
>
> When either of my two sons would start to fight, I'd walk in, separate them and say, "You have to be nice to each other." I felt that my husband's remoteness and moodiness would go away if only I could be sweet enough and do whatever he wanted.

In my first therapy session, I felt Dr. Montgomery had x-ray eyes that looked right inside me. I mentioned that I'd undergone gall bladder surgery at thirty-five years of age. He suggested that "gall" means irritation or annoyance—a bitter angry feeling—and that perhaps my gall bladder had stored up a lifetime of vile feelings until it had to be taken out. My overeating had served the purpose of stuffing my feelings.

When he said my unconscious was filled with fury from the years of holding in my real feelings, I suddenly saw the truth. A wave of relief swept over me. I felt hope for the first time. Now it was time to face my emotions directly and learn to express them.

My therapy lasted once a week for six months. The idea of the compass of the self clicked immediately. I began to catch myself when I was stuck on the love pole, swallowing my anger instead of expressing it. Then I'd try to stretch from the love pole to the assertion pole by telling the person how I really felt, even if they'd get upset with me. I learned that my mental health required both honesty and courage. Sometimes I went overboard, where I would verbally attack my husband or yell at the kids. At those times I found I could swing back into the love pole to ask forgiveness or make amends.

By the third month of growth and change, my depression lifted. I began to feel free to express love, assertion, weakness or strength without being servile or ashamed of myself. It was wonderful to no longer be held hostage to other people's opinions. My playfulness began to surface. I laughed more and became more sexually responsive to my husband. After decades of living with a straight jacket of reserve that practically kept me from breathing, I finally felt the joy of being my real self!

An old friend who hadn't seen me for a year said that she didn't recognize me. We went out for dinner on Friday night and she said, "Natalie, you're so alive now, like you've finally come home to yourself." I knew she was right.

The attitude of the person stuck on the love compass point is "Please love me; please support me; please approve of me." In the *dependent personality perspective,* our thoughts run like this:

- others need to make my important decisions for me
- I need to agree with people so they'll like me
- in a crisis, someone needs to take care of me
- I need continuous support and advice
- I can't function without constant reassurance
- if someone isn't cheerful toward me, I know they don't like me
- I should never say no to people's requests
- if I can find an all-loving, all-powerful partner, then my life will be happy

In the dependent perspective, we hobble through life pleasing and placating everyone. Father Richard McBrien writes: "The virtue of fortitude is missing in a person who is always fearful of displeasing others, who remains silent in the face of injustice, who shuns conflict at all costs, who avoids 'rocking the boat,' and who, therefore, does whatever he or she thinks is 'expected.'"[7]

Being stuck on the love polarity makes us interpersonally naive and vulnerable to manipulation by top dog personalities—people who use the strength and assertive compass points, but lack love and humility.

Signs of Unbalanced Dependency

At a women's conference, a forty-year-old woman came up to me with tears in her eyes. She said my discussion of the dependent style described her perfectly. "My father always treated me like a little girl and my mother always told me to obey him. But he never showed me love or affection. He just gave me orders. Then I married a man just like him. My husband never asks what I want or need. He just gives me orders and finds fault with what I do. What hurts the most is that my church has taught me the same thing—that I am supposed to serve everybody and never think of myself!"

The dependent pattern of loving traps us into a little boy or little girl mentality. It blocks the development of our adult capacities for thinking, choosing and coping.

As Christians we constantly hear how important it is to love and serve. We hear how Christ loved us so much that he died for our sins. We hear how the Holy Spirit can fill our hearts with love so that we can be an inspiration to others. So how can loving be wrong?

The dependent pattern of loving traps us into a little boy or little girl mentality. It blocks the development of our adult capacities for thinking, choosing and coping. We are devastated by someone's rejection of us. We constantly second-guess ourselves, for fear of incurring someone's displeasure or disapproval. We live with the anxiety that we'll make a mistake if we stand on our own two feet. We submit to authority figures or authoritarian institutions to feel a sense of security. Even our friends and children can control our self-worth. We don't know how to love ourselves and even consider it selfish to do so. We only know how to please and placate others.

Father van Kaam writes:

> When I experience a strong need for affection and approval in my spiritual life, I should be suspicious about the wholesomeness of my motives. For example, I may feel a need to please those who are my spiritual directors or models, such as the priests of my parish, the clergyman who is the director of a religious organization to which I belong, my novice master or mistress, my superior or my fellow religious.... Even my relation to God may be permeated by this neurotic need for approval.[8]

These warning signs tell us that we are functioning from the Dependent Perspective:

1. We place our worth in other people's hands. We want to know what *they* think we should do and whether they approve of every step we take. We care too much about whether they like us or not.

2. Our extreme outer-direction results in a lack of personal identity. If we have constant support and encouragement, we can be cheerful. But whenever that support wavers, we become depressed.

3. We are naive and gullible. We have a blind faith in authority figures. We fear conflict with anyone. We bend over backward to keep the peace and make others happy with us.

4. We are fixated at the infantile level of always needing help and approval. We are still connected to others by a psychological umbilical cord. We can't stand on our own feet and take responsibility for ourselves.

5. We avoid our strength and assertion poles. We overly exaggerate love in the forms of pleasing, placating and complying. We are fearful of disappointing anyone's expectations.

6. Pay us a compliment and we quickly forget it. Give us a criticism and we feel hurt for days.//
7. We strive to please God by being sweet, nice and good. We prefer to believe that no one is truly evil, that everything will work out fine if we just trust and obey.
8. As dependents, we are fortunate if we actually find a partner who has both strength and love. More often, though—because of our lack of discernment about people—we are drawn to a partner who is strong but lacks empathy, who is aggressive but lacks love.

When we live with a desperate need for people's approval, we make them our Lord. We empower them to determine our self-worth and tell us how to live. Because we make them our judge and jury, we always feel on trial. We try to convince them we are okay, but feel guilty for not meeting their expectations. Spiritually, we do not have enough presence of mind to follow Jesus as our Lord. His guidance might bring us into human conflict and that's the last thing we want. So we define our spirituality as being obedient to religious authorities and following all the rules.

But the truth is that Christians are not in the world to live up to everyone's expectations. Christ lived beyond people's approval or disapproval, solely concerned with doing the Father's will. Why assume that everybody else knows more than the Holy Spirit? Why not develop our own courage and discernment in following our inner truth in Christ? Why not negotiate for change instead of putting up with bad situations forever? We can choose to outgrow the dependent pattern.

Turning Dependency Around

A priest referred Mark and Judy to me for counseling. Mark wore a three-piece-suit with a bright red tie to our first session. His eyes probed both me and my office. He mentioned straight away that angel fish would be a better choice for my aquarium than gold fish. After sitting down, he explained, "If Judy would just obey me and be happy, things would be fine."

Judy's paste-on smile seemed out of sync with the despair in her blue eyes. She avoided eye contact with me and gazed at the floor instead. I suspected that Mark and Judy were neither friends nor lovers, that the balance in their marriage was entirely out of whack.

"I work hard as an attorney," said Mark. "Judy gets to stay home with the kids and have free time all day. She shouldn't be depressed. She should be thankful for all the money I make. I even take her on a vacation every year."

"We only go where you want to go," Judy whispered.

"That's because I earn the money!" retorted Mark. I doubted if he realized how harsh his voice sounded.

"Judy," I said, "are there times when you express a desire to vacation somewhere and Mark overrules you?"

"He's done that for the twelve years we've been married," she said, twisting a Kleenex in her hands. "Whenever I suggest a place, he lectures me about why it's a bad choice. Then we go wherever he wants to go."

"Dr. Montgomery," said Mark with growing agitation, "this is what I hate about Judy. She's never happy."

Judy slumped down. She'd been overruled again.

I raised my hands to signal a time-out. "Mark, I want to ask you an important question. *Do you love Judy?*"

He looked indignant. "Of course I love her. Why do you think I married her? Why do you think I'm paying for this counseling!"

I turned to her. "Judy, what are you feeling as Mark says how much he loves you?"

Her body squirmed as though on a skewer. "I don't know. I'm afraid to say what I really feel—" Her voice trailed away and her eyes glanced downward. I waited for her to finish. Mark fidgeted and strained to keep from finishing her sentence for her.

Judy looked up with a pained smile. Tears welled up in her eyes. "He's a good provider," she said.

Mark didn't notice the tearing. "See, I told you I love her!" He glanced at his watch.

I turned back to Judy. "Judy, the words you just said sounded hollow. Your eyes are tearing and your Kleenex is in shreds. I want to ask my question in a different way: Do you *feel loved* by Mark?"

Judy began crying. Mark looked abashed. He checked his watch again. I assured him that Judy would calm down as soon as she'd let out her pain. At the peak of her sobbing, Judy cried out, *"I don't feel loved...I haven't felt loved in all these years!"*

Gradually, Judy regained her composure. She looked at Mark. Her voice showed new strength. "You always put yourself first," she said. "You think you know everything. You give me lectures. I can't ever please you."

I slipped a third Kleenex into her hand. "Judy," I said, "it's good to express yourself honestly. Can you tell Mark how you really feel about your marriage?"

"All right," she said, looking at Mark. "Here's the truth. There are two people in this marriage—you and you. I'm sick to death of being treated like a little girl. I'm an adult woman. I want you to respect what I say."

Mark loosened his tie. His face flushed.

"Mark," I said, "do you want a happy marriage or a damaged one?"

"A happy one," he said quietly.

"Are you willing to listen to Judy, even if it goes against your grain?"

He nodded.

"Would you tell Judy what you just heard her say?" I asked.

He looked at her. "You said I'm selfish and don't respect you."

"That's good," I coached him. "Now Judy, how does it feel when Mark listens instead of lecturing you?"

She gazed at him. "It feels different for Mark to actually hear me—it feels good."

Mark eased back in his chair, his eyes growing moist. "I never knew Judy was in this much pain. I really do love her. I just never knew how to show it."

I offered a healing prayer to God to conclude our first session. "Father, you've seen the pain in this marriage. Mark and Judy are willing to develop a more balanced relationship. Show Mark how to develop more empathy and affection. Help Judy increase her assertion and self-confidence. In Jesus' name. Amen."

Over the next fifteen weeks of counseling, Judy no longer swallowed her emotions. She learned to express opinions, ideas and feelings. For his part, Mark became more skilled at listening to Judy, and respecting her honest input. He became willing to show his love for Judy openly.

With God's help, Judy shed her dependent perspective, and she learned the rhythm between love and assertion.

Anger Is a Normal Feeling

All people feel angry from time to time. The Lord expressed anger and irritation on a number of occasions. Anger is a natural and important feeling, because human beings sometimes act as sandpaper—rubbing each other the wrong way. We need to say "Ouch," or "I resent that." Diplomatic confrontation allows us to be calmly assertive without plunging into threats, intimidation or violence.

Anger that is not honestly acknowledged or expressed comes out in unconscious and destructive ways. For instance, a man gets mad at his boss for not giving him a raise. He keeps smiling in order not to rock the boat. He goes home and yells at his wife for cooking dinner wrong. His wife displaces her anger onto the children by lecturing them for not putting their toys away. The children in turn kick their dog out of their room. The dog bites the family cat. The cat sulks in a corner, wishing it didn't live in such a crazy household. All of this displaced anger causes confusion and hurt feelings, with no gains for anyone. The man would have been wiser to express his feelings directly to his boss.

Father van Kaam writes: "When I feel angry, I must not smile sweetly or freeze sullenly. I must learn instead to be humble and courageous enough to let my feelings out—straight, honestly, and simply, yet wisely and not destructively.... Surprisingly, when I learn to communicate my feelings at their first emergence to those whom I can trust, it will become easier for me to express them in a modest and relaxed manner, which may restore the atmosphere of gentleness."[9]

Holding anger inside can wreck our marriages, confuse our children, alienate co-workers and interfere with following the Lord. The rhythm between assertion and love allows each of us to be our real selves and at the same time be honest with others.

Diplomatic Assertion

Here is a rule of thumb for self-expression. Any feeling which persists over time in a relationship that you care about needs to be expressed. Choose an appropriate time. Warm-up the other person in a friendly manner. Express yourself without exaggeration or apology. After you've expressed your feelings calmly and honestly, relax and hear how the other person responds. The openness to genuine encounter reverses dependency and opens the door to identity, intimacy and community.

We know we have outgrown our dependent pattern when we are able to assert ourselves in the following ways:

- being honest with others
- expressing our feelings
- challenging manipulation
- saying no to things we do not choose to do

- standing up for our right to disagree, question authority or negotiate for fair play
- practicing responsible self-direction, while remaining open to the Holy Spirit to influence, correct and guide us

A priest wrote me from India, "While reading your material on the dependent perspective, I found I was suffering from it, especially needing everyone's approval and being too shy to assert myself. Through prayer, reflection and effort, I am facing and overcoming these tendencies. It is a joy to find that God loves the real me!"

PRACTICAL GROWTH STRETCHES

1. Dependents are afraid to express their personal tastes, desires and preferences. This week disclose to several people your favorite color, food, music or hobby. Dare to express yourself so that you will be visible to others and allow them to know the real you.

2. Challenge your fear of making waves. In conversation this week clearly state your own opinion or belief on a topic. You can disagree while remaining loyal to your friendships. Others will begin to understand and respect your point of view.

3. Observe friends who can diplomatically assert themselves. Picture yourself acting the same way. Model their healthy assertion until your own spontaneous style develops. Give yourself a test at the end of the week: tactfully negotiate for something you really want in a calm but firm manner.

4. Handle someone's disapproval of you this week. Tell yourself that you are not in the world to live up to their expectations. Refuse to feel guilty about being true to yourself. Ask Christ to strengthen your self-identity so you can stand up for yourself without fear.

5. Make an independent decision and follow it through. Sign up for a community college class, buy something nice for yourself,

join a health spa or plan a vacation. Resist the temptation to ask for other people's opinions. Take responsibility for decisions that are right for you.

6. Ponder the following scriptures. Ask the Holy Spirit to help apply them to your personality growth. Record your insights in your prayer diary.

> Romans 12:2—*Do not be conformed to this world but be transformed by the renewal of your mind, that you may prove what is the will of God, what is good and acceptable and perfect.*
>
> Proverbs 4:5-6—*Get wisdom; get insight. Do not forsake her, and she will keep you; love her, and she will guard you.*
>
> Matthew 10:16—*Be wise as serpents and innocent as doves.*
>
> Galatians 1:10—*And am I now seeking the favor of men, or of God? Or am I trying to please men? If I were still pleasing men, I should not be a servant of Christ.*

7. Breathe deeply from your belly when you feel fearful of self-expression. Repeat the words, "I can be my real self. God loves me just as I am."

Five

The Aggressive Christian
(Assertion Compass Point)

O RLANDO HAD BEEN FIGHTING A LOSING battle over anxiety and anger, his body so riddled with tension that he couldn't sleep at night. His priest had referred him for counseling. Before long I uncovered a major source of his distress: Orlando hated his older brother.

When they were growing up, Hector cruelly called his younger brother a bastard. He also beat him up several times, accentuating the shame that Orlando already felt in being the only stepchild in a large family. When they entered elementary school, Hector told other kids to call his brother a bastard. Only too happy to comply, many of them tormented the boy for years.

When he came to see me for therapy, Orlando related these traumas with hot tears and doubled-up fists. These two brothers were now in their forties. Even though Hector lay in the hospital dying from cancer, Orlando refused to write or visit because of the resentment left from childhood.

Orlando agreed with me that this toxic inner bitterness blocked his way to happiness. I suggested that he make a serious attempt to get over his hatred of Hector. This grown man shook his head vehemently. "It's impossible, Dr. Dan! I hate him too much. He deserves to die. God forgive me, I hope he goes straight to hell!"

Nevertheless, Orlando was *willing to become willing* to let go of the hate if he could be shown a way. I asked him to picture Hector in an empty chair across from us. I told him to pour out all his old resentments, to tell his older brother exactly how he felt.

Orlando started sweating as he glared at the empty chair. Then he fired out a dozen instances where Hector had abused and humiliated him. He breathed hard; his eyes blazed with anger. I complimented Orlando on his emotional honesty and pointed out that therapy was a safe place to let this dam of resentment burst. No harm came to Hector through Orlando's rage. We paused so that Orlando could relax and realize that a deep reservoir of negative emotions had opened up and flowed through him during this brief encounter with Hector's image.

Then we moved into the second phase of his emotional cleansing: gaining a new perspective. I asked Orlando to picture Hector in the hospital on his death bed. I asked him to take a few moments and tell Hector something positive—anything at all that was *good* about Hector. Orlando winced. "There's *nothing* good about Hector!" he yelled.

I rephrased the question. Had Hector ever been good to anyone else? Finally Orlando nodded. He closed his eyes and spoke to his older brother in the imagined hospital scene: "Hector, you did a good job taking care of Mom when her husband left her. You also did good starting the volunteer fire department in town and saving a couple of people's lives." Then Orlando looked at me. "That's it," he declared.

That was enough to pop the cork out of the bottleneck of Orlando's aggressive perspective. Now the transformation from negativity to a positive life could begin. We had generated *spiritual movement* by dislodging the boulder of hatred from his core. Now the Holy Spirit could bring new emotions to the fore. Orlando was taking the necessary risks to exchange his pride and hatred for forgiveness and compassion.

"How do you feel about your brother now?" I asked.

"He's still a jerk and I don't want to see him."

"That is a *thought*. What do you *feel* inside? Search your heart for any new emotion."

"I guess I feel sorry for him since he's going to die," Orlando finally answered.

"Good. That is a feeling. It's called compassion. Now I want to show you how to act on that new feeling."

"I'm not going to go see him!" my client protested.

"No, you don't have to until you want to. I want you to do something else. I want you to pray for him. I want you to ask God to forgive Hector."

"I can't pray for him. He's a mean man and an atheist."

"That doesn't matter. Get off your high horse and give it a try. You don't have to *like* him. Just ask God to help him."

"I'll try. But I don't think you can pray for somebody you hate."

"Do you want to be healed?"

Orlando nodded.

"Then go ahead and give it a try," I said.

We bowed our heads. "Dear God," said Orlando. "Please help Hector in the hospital. He helped Mom a lot and he helped the people in town. He's going to die and he needs you. Please go to his room and bless him. Amen." By the time he had finished praying, tears were streaming down his cheeks.

"That was beautiful, Orlando," I said. "Why are you crying?"

"Because I'm afraid God is going to go over there and heal him," he laughed.

"Why else?"

"I guess because I want God to bless him after all. Maybe I'll go over there myself. Mom is the only one who goes to visit him."

"Sometimes God uses us to answer our own prayers," I said. "Anyway, you're back in emotional contact with yourself and with your brother. Don't be surprised if feelings of love come up. You guys may have a chance for a relationship yet. Just do the next right thing."

To harbor resentment for years, to blame someone for our unhappiness, to hate our neighbor—these are the traps of the aggressive perspective. The attitude of people stuck on the assertion compass point is: "Others are to blame for my misfortunes. I can't trust anybody. People whom I dislike should go to hell." In the aggressive perspective, the thoughts which rule our behavior are the opposite of dependency:

- I can do whatever I want regardless of the consequences to others
- might makes right
- love is sloppy sentimentality
- weakness is despicable and should be scorned
- the meaning of life is self-interest
- the highest good is what I want right now
- people are untrustworthy
- it pays to be suspicious
- people are out to get me
- people who have wronged me deserve my hatred

Aggressives Believe They Own You

Aggressives are unable to sustain intimate or enduring relationships because they are always blowing up. They are stuck on the assertion compass point with exaggerated aggression. They lack humility from the weakness pole, kindness from the love pole, and esteem from the strength pole of personality.

The best single adjective to describe the person caught in the spell of the aggressive perspective is *sadistic*. I have in mind no sexual connotation. Aggressives delight in humiliating others or lording power over them. They entertain themselves by picking on people.

Their jokes have barbs. They elevate themselves by putting others down. They wreak havoc in family life or religious communities and blame their divisiveness and strife on others.

Father van Kaam writes: "I may seek for power within the religious organization of which I am a member, as a layman, a priest, or a religious. I may crave power for its own sake, not for the sake of the religious community or of the faithful. Moreover, my personal spiritual life may be marked by my addiction to power."[10]

Aggressives try to convince you that what you do is wrong, what you think is stupid and what you feel is silly.

Aggressives love to prick bubbles. If you have good news, they're disinterested. If you're trying something new, they broadcast your mistakes. If you achieve something, they put it down. If you show joy or happiness, they rain on your parade. Aggressives try to convince you that what you do is wrong, what you think is stupid and what you feel is silly.

In my early twenties, I belonged to a singing ensemble that was ministering to churches in several states. We trusted the Lord to make ends meet and often stayed in the homes of people from the churches where we sang. One night I was assigned to a family of a deacon in the church. The couple's thirty-year-old daughter, Sandy, was visiting home over the weekend. I was about to see an aggressive parent in action.

During a wonderful dinner, I noticed the wife eyeing her husband nervously. Halfway through the meal, the daughter mentioned she'd be graduating with her Ph.D. in the spring. She said she might try writing a book soon. I started to congratulate her, but her father cut me short.

"Sandy, don't give Mr. Montgomery the impression that you're smart, because you're not. You don't know anything about life, and I'd never read anything you wrote! You're just a little dummy with your head screwed on backward!"

Sandy's face turned scarlet. She shoved her plate aside and raced out the front door. I heard her car start and that was the last I saw of her. We finished the meal in silence. That night my heart ached for Sandy. I asked God her heavenly Father to counter the aggressive trends of her earthly father. I hoped the Holy Spirit would somehow build up her self-esteem and give her joy at graduation.

The Aggressive Style

When stuck on the assertion polarity, we judge, attack and ventilate on those around us, making them scapegoats of our discontent. We may charm outsiders but pour rage on family members. The following symptoms characterize the aggressive style of personality imbalance:

1. We view life as a dog-eat-dog world. If we don't get our way, we make plans to get even. We hold grudges for years. We trust no one but ourselves. The main emotions we feel are bitterness, spite and hatred.

2. We harm others without feeling guilty. We say to ourselves, "They had it coming!" We view spouses and children as our private possessions, often becoming furious if they don't obey our strict rules.

3. We are stubborn and proud of it. Our views are always right. We have nothing to learn and are suspicious of anyone who might teach us something. We consider the views of others as irrelevant to our decisions.

4. We intimidate others with icy glares, raised eyebrows, pointed fingers, cold shoulders and long lectures. We may

threaten abandonment or physical violence in order to make them shape up. We are masters at controlling people through fear. We like to argue and are quick to take offense over the slightest issue.

5. We can be quite charming if this gets us what we want. We take pride in pulling the wool over people's eyes. We hide our motives and gloat over our victories. We are tough-minded realists who know how to watch out for ourselves. We live life on *our* terms.

6. If someone threatens us, we get stronger. If someone criticizes us, we get meaner. If someone humiliates us, we get even. Nobody messes with us.

7. We conceal our shortcomings and problems because they're nobody's business. We believe that others gloat over our weaknesses. We keep our hearts like stone so that no one can hurt us.

8. We are unwilling to "give in," even on trivial issues, because we consider compromise a sign of weakness.

9. Frequently, we are insanely jealous of our spouses and use this to interrogate them. Any time they're out of our sight we grow suspicious, always assuming betrayal. We demand to know where they are at all times. We isolate them and threaten harsh punishments if they don't stay in line.

10. If we are religious, we believe that God is an angry God. Like us, God hates the weak, soft or defective. We feel his wrath toward all who are different from us. We serve God by threatening people so that they will obey us.

The tragic reality of the aggressive, writes Karen Horney, is that "his resentment, his devaluing attitude gives rise to a permanent feeling of disappointment and discontent.... Since it does not occur to him that the sources of his chronic discontent could lie within himself, he feels entitled to impress upon others how they fail him and to make ever greater demands whose fulfillment can never satisfy him."[11]

Scripture censures the destructive mode of the aggressive perspective:

- Proverbs 19:19—*A man of great wrath will pay the penalty; for if you deliver him, you will only have to do it again.*
- Proverbs 15:1—*A soft answer turns away wrath, but a harsh word stirs up anger.*
- Galatians 5:19—*Now the works of the flesh are plain: fornication, impurity, licentiousness, idolatry, sorcery, enmity, strife, jealousy, anger, selfishness, dissension, party spirit, envy, drunkenness, carousing, and the like.*
- Ephesians 6:4—*Fathers, do not provoke your children to anger, but bring them up in the discipline and instruction of the Lord.*
- James 1:20—*For the anger of man does not work the righteousness of God.*

Even though aggression brings much evil into the world, there is still hope. All spiritual shortcomings and partial perspectives can be redeemed and transformed. Aggressive Christians can choose to outgrow their impatience, vindictiveness and tendency to enslave others. This requires great courage, because it is far more difficult to love people than to feel angry toward them. It is harder to love than to disparage.

Growth stretches into the weakness and love compass points change aggression into healthy assertion.

How to Balance Aggressive Trends

Nathaniel came across as verbally aggressive with his wife, secretary and office workers. I picked up on his aggressive tendencies in our first session.

As a chief hospital administrator, Nat prided himself on making people walk on eggshells. "When I crack the whip, people jump!" he bragged.

I suggested to Nat that his bullying ways were costing him dearly. His wife had become emotionally distant and sexually disinterested; three different secretaries quit within a year; and his fellow office workers hated his guts.

Nat defended himself. "Everybody's a slacker at work. If I don't chew them out, they'll take advantage of me. As for my wife, she just wants an easy ride. I've got to stay on her case to make her behave."

It's not easy to make people aware that their own unhealthy attitudes are making their lives miserable or harming those around them. I used an indirect approach with Nat. He spoke about how people were afraid of him. I reframed this, "You like to see people grovel because they're afraid you'll blow your stack."

He spoke about special privileges he took at the hospital. I said, "You like to play the prima donna and lord it over everyone."

He mentioned how he had ripped his secretary apart that very day. "You feel powerful when you make mountains out of molehills," I said.

Nat became irritated with these reflections.

"Dr. Dan, you're painting a picture of me that isn't exactly pretty. What are you driving at?"

"Nat, I'm mirroring what you're saying about yourself."

"So what's the bottom line?" he asked, taking out a handkerchief to wipe the sweat off his hands.

"I prefer that you tell me."

"That I'm a jerk?" Nat offered.

"Excellent," I said. "That's the most accurate insight you've had so far!"

Nat struggled for months with the process of developing a balanced personality. Yet, he made discernible progress. A year later, his wife told me of her happiness with Nat's hard-earned turn-around.

The office workers threw a surprise party for their boss. One woman said, "Nat, you've changed so much. You're not a troll anymore."

To outgrow aggressive trends, we need to:

- challenge and change our cynicism
- make amends to those we've hurt or harmed
- honestly admit our shortcomings
- consider anger a luxury we cannot afford
- ask for help when we need it
- handle people's criticisms without defensiveness
- live and let live
- value individual differences
- grow in tolerance, patience and compassion for ourselves and others
- choose to trust others and give them the benefit of the doubt
- learn to focus on God's love and mercy

Expressing Love and Nurturance

Expressing the love end of the love/assertion polarity transforms the aggressive perspective toward wholeness. The person learns to say and feel such phrases as "I'm interested," "I'm attracted," "I care," and "I care tenderly." This restores the growth process of personality and stimulates a new openness to the Holy Spirit.

In Keith Miller's book, *Please Love Me,* Hedy Robinson speaks of how many family members long for a balance of love and assertion in the home:

I couldn't help wondering if there weren't families somewhere in which people told each other every day about the love they felt and hugged and kissed each other, where people shared their hopes and dreams, their difficulties and fears at the dining room table. I tried to imagine our doing that, but couldn't. As long as I could remember, I'd wanted to express my feelings of love and affection to people close to me. But the greater fear of being rejected always kept me from it.[12]

Love chained inside is love lost. Love expressed openly is love made actual. To share love is the greatest experience a human being can know. Aggressives who take the risk of loving and being vulnerable find the satisfaction that formerly eluded them.

Psychologist Rollo May writes: "The rigid bonds of his selfishness are broken down by a taste of the gratification of unselfishness. Joy wells up and streams over his pain. And love comes into the man's life to vanquish his loneliness.... Such is the transformation from neurosis to personality health. And such is what it means, likewise, to experience religion."[13]

PRACTICAL GROWTH STRETCHES

1. Examine your own life for a minute. Are you willing to put away anger and surrender your need to control others? Are you willing to feel excited about other people's joy and to be supportive in their times of need? Will you tell family and friends that you love them? Will you back up your words with concrete actions of generosity and interest? Can you begin this week by offering hugs, pats on the shoulder and smiles?

2. An antagonistic attitude and a hair-trigger temper are enemies of the spiritual life. Smash the illusion that your anger is necessary. Review your life history and write down instances where your anger has burned bridges with family and associates. Make amends

where possible. Stop blaming others for your personality defects. Instead, ask yourself: "How can I see this situation differently? How can I hear the other person's view? How can I express humility, patience or caring?"

3. Talk to a friend or a professional counselor about any wounds you received in childhood. Were you humiliated, abused or criticized by a family member or sibling? Were your early attempts to receive love rebuffed? Talk openly about your anxiety, weakness and pain—this is the opposite of aggressive defensiveness.

4. Whenever you start becoming suspicious and spiteful, stop in your tracks and pray for the Holy Spirit to give you a more positive outlook. Be generous to a fault. Give a gift without expecting repayment. Fulfill a promise joyfully. Remember someone's birthday, anniversary or graduation by sending a nice card. Bring cheer and comfort to someone in the hospital. Discover the pleasures of being a positive person.

5. Focus on genuine service rather than getting your way. Serve in a soup kitchen, volunteer in a day care center, become a Big Brother or Big Sister or teach a class at your parish. Ask God to fill you with the Holy Spirit, so you can share in the humility and compassion of our Lord.

Six

The Withdrawn Christian
(Weakness Compass Point)

A YOUNG WOMAN NAMED TINA CAME to me for therapy. She spoke so softly in our sessions that I could barely hear her. Tina loved children and animals, but other adults terrified her. Like a fawn wounded by a hunter's bullet, she was skittish, hypersensitive and avoidant. She longed to be healed, but greatly feared disclosing herself to me. Tina seemed to assume rejection. Disparagement from men was all she'd ever known.

Early in therapy I identified the negative self-talk that automatically played in Tina's mind. "I'm inadequate." "I don't fit in." "I'm ugly." "I don't have anything to offer." "If anyone really knew me, they'd reject me." "If others criticize me, they must be right." "It's better not to try anything than to risk trying and fail."

Where could such thoughts originate? It took ten weeks before Tina whispered the shameful secret revealing how her spiritual core had been clogged during childhood.

"When I was six, my uncle...."

I knew the rest. She didn't even have to finish the ugly story, which I'd heard all too often from other victims of sexual abuse. Tina's father had abandoned the family when she was five. Her mother became withdrawn and helpless, modeling how to hide from life rather than deal with it. When Tina was six, the vulnerable little girl became a prime target for her uncle, who molested her regularly until she was nine. Tina's shame had kept her from telling anyone until the day she finally told me.

Even God, she felt, judged her as nasty and evil for letting such a terrible thing happen. Tina's life script came to be "I am an evil person who deserves punishment. I deserve to be shamed and isolated. I am a social leper. I might as well be dead."

I arranged for a psychiatrist who lived in her town to put Tina on anti-depressant medication during the first year of psychotherapy. The drug helped to remove her suicidal impulses. For someone suffering major depression, such a medication can be advisable and even necessary. After the fog of despair begins to lift from the mind and physical vitality is bolstered, personality rigidities can be more easily faced and resolved.

During the first few months of therapy, Tina brought me drawings which illustrated her inner agony and poor self-image. One captured Tina's suicidal urges by showing a severed head being carried in her hand. Another drawing portrayed her identity confusion—two hands covering a face peek-a-boo style. Tina's painful helplessness was depicted in many pictures of women in various fetal positions. A powerful drawing illuminated her despair and unconscious hope for resurrection—a dead woman with an Easter lily growing out of her belly.

Our weekly therapy slowly awakened her instincts for self-preservation and self-esteem. Tina and I worked through the sexual abuse memories and nightmares until they stopped plaguing her.

I pointed out to Tina that she could speed up her recovery by developing a more balanced personality and I explained the compass of the self. Instead of exaggerating her use of *weakness*, she needed to focus on all the compass points—love, assertion, weakness and strength. I encouraged Tina to risk new behaviors that would serve as opportunities for growth.

Before long Tina began to get her bearings. She learned to express herself calmly and clearly, to expand her artistic talents in commercial directions, and to gain personal identity and intimacy with others. Tina's intuitions and hunches became more reliable. Her trust in the still, small voice of the Lord increased.

Whenever Tina demonstrated creative thinking, emotional expression, or assertive problem-solving, I heaped her with accolades. I cheered her on enthusiastically. This abused woman needed to know that she was not alone, that God and I were squarely in her corner. I continued to praise her intelligence, sensitivity and enterprising spirit until she had internalized these positive evaluations of herself.

Tina showed promise as an artist. In the final phase of therapy I coached her to set up a studio, negotiate professional fees and deal with clients confidently. Suddenly, through an inspired period of creativity, a dozen color drawings poured out of her. These gorgeous, sensitive pieces included a fawn in the woods, a little girl playing with a butterfly, a group of swans swimming, an eagle in flight and a child laughing.

One which especially touched me was a rendition of baby Jesus being visited by a squirrel, a fawn, a mouse, a duck, a raccoon, a sparrow and a butterfly. This cascade of artistic expression demonstrated that at last her artesian well flowed fully and freely. The gift of Tina's pain became a fountainhead of creativity filling her with the Holy Spirit and joy.

Tina hasn't forgotten her dark years of quiet desperation—the silent aching of her soul and the near fatal clogging of her inner core. Now she is an accomplished wildlife artist, an author and illustrator of children's books and a public speaker. She witnesses to the hope that by integrating the compass of the self with the grace of God, we can develop a balanced personality.

We All Feel Anxiety and Weakness

People stuck on the weakness compass point ache silently for relief without finding it. The attitude of the person stuck on the weakness pole becomes "I am a social misfit. People are too much trouble. Life is unfulfilling. I may as well give up." In the *withdrawn personality perspective* we find the following beliefs at work:

- people do not like or accept me
- I don't need close friends or confidants
- I need to be left to myself at home and at work
- risks are not worth taking; they never turn out right
- life should be structured and highly predictable
- I am different; I don't fit in
- I don't have anything to say to people
- I make a fool of myself when I try something new
- if people really knew me, they wouldn't like me
- life is less complicated without other people
- human relationships are not worth the bother

Human beings have a deep, instinctive need to be loved and affirmed. When we are discounted instead, we experience worry, doubt, hurt and anxiety. Anxiety is the most universal of all these emotional negatives. I've learned in years of counseling that we all feel anxiety. The only difference is that people stuck on the weakness compass point forge anxiety into a way of life.

Psychiatrist Paul Tournier writes of the withdrawn perspective:

Neurosis, shyness, feelings of inferiority, lack of self-confidence, hypersensitivity, pathological feelings of guilt, emotional instability, obsessions, panic, functional disturbances, indecision, and depression are the expression of weak reactions. In their turn, all these unhealthy manifestations maintain in the subject a feeling of weakness which provokes him to further weak reactions.[14]

The following behaviors may alert us to the withdrawn perspective in our personality.

1. We are blocked from initiating friendships with others. We long to be liked, but are convinced that we are unlikeable. We watch for the slightest sign of rejection. Our most common feelings are futility and a sense of numbness. That is, we shut down all emotions so that we don't feel anything.

2. We are shy, timid and hypersensitive. We fantasize that people feel negatively toward us. We are prone to feelings of inferiority, panic attacks, shame, sadness, self-pity and hopelessness.

3. We are so preoccupied with fears and insecurities that we constantly imagine that we are in danger. We always pursue the course of greatest safety, which is to take no risks whatever. We draw an *imaginary circle* around ourselves which no one can penetrate.

4. We are a basket case of "nerves" around people. We often experience palpitations, sweating, blushing, or stomach cramps. In social situations we "shut down" by standing in the corner or leaving at the first opportunity. Our minds can go blank if we are called upon to speak. We avoid direct eye contact at all costs. Only by *active withdrawal* can we protect ourselves. Only in being alone do we gain a sense of relief.

5. Our goals are negative: not to be involved; not to need anyone; not to allow others to influence us; not to care.

6. We discount compliments by believing that people are putting us on. They are setting us up for ridicule, or else they just don't know how inadequate we really are.

7. Since our attempts at bonding in the past have only brought us misery, we repress and constrain our desires for affection. Life is a party that we fear to attend.

8. Equally uncomfortable is our relationship with God. Even

though we may believe in him, we are convinced that he doesn't like us. We feel that God would accept the whole world before he would choose us as friends, that he despises us because of our weaknesses, that he knows what cowards and failures we are. We believe that God is ashamed of us.

Father van Kaam writes: "Another result of neurotic understanding of spiritual life may be the restriction of my life within limits which are unreasonably narrow. I shall not demand anything even if I need it badly. I shall be content with as little as possible and make a fetish of being modest, unnoticed, and retiring."[15]

Moving Toward Personality Balance

Once while speaking at a religious conference, I suggested that *life is not fair; nobody owes us our dream.* This needs to be accepted up front by withdrawn individuals so they can develop the courage of perseverance and the willingness to take required risks.

Jesuit priest and spiritual director Anthony de Mello suggests in story form how important it is for people to develop their full personality potential:

> A man found an eagle's egg and put it in a nest of a barnyard hen. The eaglet hatched with the brood of chicks and grew up with them.
>
> All his life the eagle did what the barnyard chicks did, thinking he was a barnyard chicken. He scratched the earth for worms and insects. He clucked and cackled. And he would thrash his wings and fly a few feet into the air.
>
> Years passed and the eagle grew very old. One day he saw a magnificent bird above him in the cloudless sky. It glided in graceful majesty among the powerful wind currents, with scarcely a beat of its strong golden wings.
>
> The old eagle looked up in awe. "Who's that?" he asked.

"That's the eagle, the king of the birds," said his neighbors. "He belongs to the sky. We belong to the earth—we're chickens." So the eagle lived and died a chicken, for that's what he thought he was.[16]

If you are a withdrawn personality, the first thing to do is to become aware of it without feeling crushed or persecuted. The second thing is to mobilize energy and commitment to make a change. The third thing is to take responsibility for making your dreams come true. On the personality compass, growth requires stretching from the weakness pole into the strength, assertion and love poles.

The celebration of your talents is a vital part of recovering from the weakness perspective.

Are you willing to give up shyness, express your real feelings and encounter others without guarantees of acceptance? Are you willing to handle criticism constructively? Are you willing to see Christ and the Holy Spirit as positive helpers who will give you strength?

The growing Christian feels gratitude, strength and self-love in the presence of the Lord. Try saying: "I am adequate," "I am capable," "I am confident," and "I am worthwhile." The celebration of your talents is a vital part of recovering from the weakness perspective. Give up the erroneous habit of seeing yourself as "stupid," "ugly," "lazy," "withdrawn" or "awkward."

Toss these negatives into the garbage pail. Choose to lay aside your inferior feelings. Enjoy the power of self-development in Christ.

Don't tolerate people, jobs and situations that feed your old inadequacy. Individuals functioning out of the withdrawn perspective have an uncanny knack for getting themselves into unbearable jobs and relationships. Don't stay in a bad situation. Use your fledgling strength to negotiate a better deal. Use your newfound courage to risk upgrading your quality of life. You have a right to express your convictions, to protest unfair treatment, to ask for help or support, to make mistakes and to negotiate for what you want and need.

Take active growth stretches that force you to relate to others. Communication skills can only be learned by communicating! Practice the art of small talk. Learn how to initiate and end conversations. Tell people how you really feel. Actively imagine yourself being more assertive. Model people you admire—practice and strengthen the skills you observe.

God's "Yes" to Our Lives

During an evening of group therapy with ten participants, an executive expressed fear of becoming alcoholic from job stress, a sister shared anxiety about a personality conflict with her superior, a wife confessed she felt terrified about her sexual attraction to another man, a parent worried about his son's rebellion, and an artist said she was afraid that she was losing her creativity. Every person felt accepted and drew strength from the warm interpersonal climate of the group.

Being a Christian does not mean that we no longer feel afraid. The Holy Spirit is with us, helping to ease our fears and to share our burdens. The Christian life is not a way "out" but a way "through" life. It takes courage to share our fears, doubts and uncertainties with God and others. But when we do so, we are comforted.

Jesus, too, experienced times of great vulnerability and pain. Consider the following scriptures: he was "very sorrowful, even to death" (Mt 26:38); he "was deeply moved in spirit and troubled" (Jn 11:33); he was "grieved" (Mk 3:5); he was "troubled" (Jn 12:27); he "wept" (Jn 11:35); and he prayed with "loud cries and tears" (Heb 5:7). In great agony of spirit he knelt in the garden of Gethsemane and prayed that the Father might spare him the dreaded ordeal ahead (Mk 14:35). He even sweat blood (Lk 22:44). The Stations of the Cross remind us of Jesus' time on the weakness compass point.

Jesus demonstrates that God's "yes" to our lives is stronger than all our negative experiences. Though he was crucified and buried, he rose again with victory in his wings. After his brief time of weakness—the passion week—the Father restored to him the joy of strength, assertion and love. In his heavenly wholeness, Christ seeks to restore our balance and serenity in the wake of human suffering.

For twenty-five years shyness and anxiety trapped Tina, whom I described earlier. Because she took small steps toward confidence and self-development, she eventually put on an art exhibit that drew a capacity crowd of two hundred. I watched with delight as she greeted people, engaged in conversation and sold her paintings for worthy prices. That day Tina told me that her old perspective of weakness seemed but a shadow life she could barely remember.

Strength enables us to become active participants and creators with God in making our dreams come true. When in touch with strength, we don't mope, murmur or whine. We take action to improve the quality of life. We take responsibility for contributing to the world around us. Your life is a spiritual adventure. Create what happens next! Commend yourself for the tiniest successes. Know that God praises your efforts too.

With growing self-confidence, obstacles become challenges and challenges turn into achievements. Shyness and avoidance become things of the past. You feel proud of the changes you make. Once you break the stranglehold of fear, nothing can hold you back again. Filled with the Holy Spirit's power, your life mission becomes unstoppable.

PRACTICAL GROWTH STRETCHES

1. Make a conscious decision to outgrow the withdrawn perspective. Pray for the Holy Spirit's assistance in transforming the defeating self-talk inside your mind. No longer repeat to yourself,

"I'm stupid," "I'm inept," "I'm not okay." Replace this self-talk with phrases like "God likes me and so do others." "God specializes in helping people like me." "Life is an adventure and from now on I'm going to show up!"

2. Dare to express your real feelings to others and to God. Start with baby steps, such as simply saying, "I'm feeling lonely"; "I'm feeling anxious"; "I'm feeling sad"; or "I'm feeling happy." A feeling is the most private, emotionally colored part of your perception. You can usually tell a genuine feeling because it's the hardest thing to share. By sharing your feelings, you come home to your core—you emotionally bond with others and discover the joy of belonging.

3. Decide to actively develop your skills, talents and potentials. Find a teacher or mentor to work with you in developing your strengths. Several years ago I decided to expand from writing books to writing magazine articles. I felt shy and awkward at first. Yet I made a phone call to a famous magazine writer and arranged for her to tutor me for several months over the phone. Within a short time, my confidence and skills blossomed. I now write for some forty magazines.

If you need intellectual or vocational assistance, sign up for college courses, adult extension classes or professional workshops. If you are an artist, hire a private tutor. If you need help with finances, child care or housing, seek out a church or community sponsored agency. With God's help, develop the desires of your heart.

4. If you still feel emotionally troubled by painful events in your past, make an appointment for pastoral counseling or psychological treatment. If you suffer from an addiction or eating disorder, join a 12 step group (phone numbers will be listed in the Yellow Pages). Work through inner conflicts so you can live effectively in the present, enjoying the fruits of a balanced personality.

5. Catch God blessing you and thank him daily. Praise yourself for your tiniest successes. Ponder the following scriptures and write down your insights in your prayer diary:

Psalm 27:1—*The Lord is my light and my salvation; whom shall I fear? The Lord is the stronghold of my life; of whom shall I be afraid?*

John 14:27—*Peace I leave with you; my peace I give to you; not as the world gives do I give to you. Let not your hearts be troubled, neither let them be afraid.*

Romans 8:28—*We know that in everything God works for good with those who love him, who are called according to his purpose.*

2 Timothy 1:7—*For God did not give us a spirit of timidity but a spirit of power and love and self-control.*

1 John 4:18—*There is no fear in love, but perfect love casts out fear. For fear has to do with punishment, and he who fears is not perfected in love.*

Isaiah 40:28-31—*Have you not known? Have you not heard? The Lord is the everlasting God, the Creator of the ends of the earth. He does not faint or grow weary, his understanding is unsearchable. He gives power to the faint, and to him who has no might he increases strength. Even youths shall faint and be weary, and young men shall fall exhausted; but they who wait for the Lord shall renew their strength, they shall mount up with wings like eagles, they shall run and not be weary, they shall walk and not faint.*

5. Practice talking to people: waitresses in restaurants; clerks in stores; the mail carrier; service station attendants; people at the spa and your spouse and kids. It doesn't matter what you say, just open your mouth and talk. You are now in contact with other human beings. Enjoy using all four compass points of your personality.

6. One way to integrate your weakness and strength compass points is to accept the paradox that both exist in you and that they are equal, like a battery with positive and negative poles. A battery will not work without the positive and negative electrical charges,

and a human personality cannot be balanced without both strength and weakness.

An example from therapy shows how one woman began to develop a healthy rhythm between weakness and strength:

Therapist: Be your lonesome self, weak.
Client: *I feel so blue and unhappy. I need a friend. (WEAKNESS)*

Therapist: Now be your opposite self, strong.
Client: *I can be my own friend. I don't need anybody else. (STRENGTH)*

Therapist: Now be the weak one again.
Client: *I'm not enough, I need others. (WEAKNESS)*

Therapist: Now be the strong one and answer.
Client: *I am enough, but I can see that having a friend would be good. (STRENGTH/WEAKNESS)*

Therapist. Be weak again.
Client: *Ok. I may not always feel that I am "enough", but I'll admit that I might be.(WEAKNESS/STRENGTH)*

Therapist: Be strong and weak.
Client: *I can decide to believe I'm enough most of the time. I can be a friend not only to myself but also to others. (STRENGTH/WEAKNESS)*

When polarities within our personality are accepted equally, the power of wholeness results.

Seven

The Controlling Christian
(Strength Compass Point)

I EARNED MY PH.D. IN MY LATE TWENTIES, by far the youngest in my graduating class. I'd read nearly a thousand books and felt proud of my accomplishments. Within the next few years, I published my first two books. While I was wise in my own eyes, I was a pain to be around.

A psychiatric facility hired me as the director of group therapy. I planned to fix everyone—and quickly. I gave lectures to the group to show them how much I knew. I offered advice to show how clever I was. I thought that I could save the world.

I had been there for about two months when an older man named Arthur remarked, "Dr. Montgomery, you've got a big ego. It really gets in your way."

That stunned me. How dare he analyze me!

A female member of the group asked if they could talk about me for a change.

I was miffed, but decided to help them out by listening. That day the group came alive for the first time. They exposed in a flash my idealized image of a know-it-all with a messiah complex.

"You have never empathized with my pain," a woman named

Sally said. "You're so obsessed with trying to control us that you're not a real person."

"You need to fix everybody to show us how great you are!" added Arthur.

"Doctor, you need some humility," seconded Sam.

On and on they talked, agreeing with one another's comments and adding to them. I sweated and blushed, sometimes trying to defend myself and sometimes listening with disbelief.

Finally, the three hours were almost up. I looked at the clock with relief.

"It's time to wind up," I said, hoping to shut them up and leave with a shred of dignity.

"Dr. Montgomery," said Sam. "I just want to say one last thing."

"Okay Sam, go ahead," I said.

"For these past two month you've been a jackass."

I left the group feeling shattered. I had entered the room the wise doctor, sent by God to save these people. Now I didn't know who I was. Worse yet, I recognized some truth in what they said. That night I wanted to resign from the hospital and leave the planet. But I decided to pray instead. I poured out my hurt and anger to the Lord. After I had finished venting, a still, small voice spoke inside me.

"Keep going back," it said. "You'll learn a lot."

Reluctantly, I crept back to the next group session. I told the people that what they had shared had shaken me. I could hear the pain in my own voice. "I'm tired of defending myself," I said. "And I'm tired of being a know-it-all. I'm going to let more of my real self out in this group, and I hope I can learn something, too."

"Thank God!" cried one woman. Then she quit focusing on me and started sharing her own pain. I felt empathy toward her for the first time.

What astonished me was that in the weeks to come, we became co-learners in the art of living. My professional input was more tempered, and balanced with self-disclosures about my own flaws and foibles. After several months, Arthur told me that sharing my weaknesses more openly had become my greatest strength.

The attitude of the person stuck on the strength compass point becomes: "I am special and other people are inferior. Everyone should admire my high standards of perfection. If I keep striving to impress others, anything is possible." In the controlling style of personality, our beliefs tend to reflect entitlement and perfectionism:

- life is a chess game—other people are pawns and I am the king
- my achievements and talents deserve special attention
- people owe me favors, but they should not expect me to pay them back
- people should admire me for my superior talents
- nobody should ever steal my limelight
- people should do things exactly as I say
- I have no use for people who do not give me compliments

Of the four partial perspectives that Christians can build into their personalities, the controlling perspective may be the most subtle.

Doesn't everyone admire the person who is strong, organized and has unshakable moral convictions? Don't we look up to people who weather every storm and overcome every obstacle?

The Christian with a controlling perspective is stuck on the strength polarity of personality. Somewhere along the line, this person got the message that work, achievement and perfection are the most important things in life.

Controllers live under the "curse of perfectionism": everything has to be done just right, which means, of course, according to their standards. Anything less than perfection requires judgment, reprimand and correction. This is why controllers are no fun to work or live with.

The controlling executive needs an efficient organizational machine which treats people like cogs in a wheel. It manipulates them as objects or statistics in order to achieve the controlling person's goals. The controlling housewife works herself to the bone, compulsively cleaning the house as though it were a museum showcase, not a home in which people enjoy being together. The perfectionist student obsesses over memorizing trivia, studying by rote and earning high grades, apart from any interest or curiosity about the subject matter.

The compulsive religious worker becomes so preoccupied with rules and regulations that he or she neglects the deeper opportunities for loving and growing in relationships with others. Unfortunately, self-awareness and sensitivity to others take a backseat to organizing and controlling them. When the Controlling Perspective runs your life, you can't help but remain a spiritual infant.

Father John Powell writes:

> I remember what a great and endless consolation it was for me to find out that the often used quotation, "be perfect as your heavenly Father"(Mt 5:48), is really a mistranslation. The context of this quotation is the challenge of Jesus to love our enemies...to be as tolerant and loving and forgiving as our heavenly Father is!
>
> I remember sitting with this scriptural passage...and I suddenly realized that God was not challenging me to be perfect, but to be patient, to be tolerant and understanding of weakness, in others and especially in myself.[17]

Two examples from Scripture underscore the point. During the Last Supper with Christ, the disciples argued over who was the most perfect: "A dispute also arose among them, which of them was to be regarded as the greatest"(Lk 22:24).

Each one of them had a unique place in the fulfillment of God's plans, but at that moment they sought to convince Jesus of their personal greatness so that one could stand out as the most important. Jesus was not interested in their claims to fame. He responded that the greatest among them would be the servant of all.

> *Without the courage*
> *to disclose our secret fears,*
> *inferiority feelings, sins,*
> *faults, doubts and hurts,*
> *we cannot make progress toward*
> *becoming a whole person.*

A second example of the perfectionist syndrome is found in Luke 9:49-50, where the disciples are again discussing who was the greatest. John said to Jesus, "Master, we saw a man casting out demons in your name, and we forbade him, because he does not follow with us." Jesus debunked this attempt at self-glorification by stating, "Do not forbid him; for he that is not against you is for you."

A major drawback to the controlling perspective is the assumption that always acting strong is a virtue, and that experiencing weakness, limitations or needs for growth is shameful. Without the courage to disclose our secret fears, inferiority feelings, sins, faults, doubts and hurts, we cannot make progress toward becoming a whole person.

What Makes Controllers Tick?

Individuals stuck with the controlling perspective focus only on winning, looking good, being admired, acquiring power and calling the shots for others.

People trapped in the controlling perspective are afraid of being judged inadequate or unworthy if they don't meet the highest standards. They do not understand the grace of God, and still struggle to impress him. Being overly serious about life, controllers scorn play, fun, humor and intimate relationships as a waste of time. Striving for perfection replaces love as the central goal of life.

The saying "God helps those who help themselves" has some wisdom. But we can use it to rationalize accomplishing and getting ahead, rather than living under grace and inspiration. The saying does not appear in the Bible.

The person with the controlling perspective attempts to appear strong, competent and capable at all times, and is in danger of becoming a workaholic. Not only that, the person dictates to others that they too should keep their noses to the grindstone.

Because controlling people are too proud to admit personal weaknesses, they are intolerant toward others. Spouses, children and colleagues especially sense a controller's constant judgment and tension. But their feedback has little impact, since the controlling individual is certain of being right.

When stuck on the strength pole, we are too self-sufficient to ask for help when we need it, too proud to say we're sorry, too competitive to be intimate, and too self-centered to listen to the needs of others. Exaggerated strength without the balance of weakness turns us into control freaks who use judgment to control others. The following symptoms can alert us that we need to restore balance in our personality:

1. We are perfectionists to the point of interfering with our ability to grasp the bigger picture. We believe that there is only one way to live and do things—our way. We judge and reject anyone or anything that doesn't comply with our standards. We are closed-minded but convinced that we know it all. We feel a need to be "junior gods."

2. We are formal in manner, stiff in carriage and proper in conversation. Our relationships reflect a tense and serious quality, even at home with family members. We are pedantic and turn life events into platforms for preaching our own morals.

3. We derive inordinate pleasure from classifying, indexing, objectifying and managing both things and people. We feel a strong need to hoard worn-out or worthless objects. We are stingy in many ways, but like to appear generous.

4. We are extremely aware of our status relative to others, which can make us dictate to subordinates and fawn on those higher up. In our families we usually opt for the dominant role. Our need to constantly teach and admonish can make our spouses feel like children and our teenagers like little boys and girls.

5. One need consumes us—to give a good impression and to be in control at all times. Our Rock of Gibraltar self-image is paramount. This keeps us from laughing, playing, feeling, risking and learning. We shun the weakness pole and shy away from the love pole.

6. We lack imagination and creativity because we rely on tradition or the rule book to prescribe what "should" be done in the present. We live mechanically by whatever is prescribed by rite, ritual and propriety. We pooh-pooh feelings and scorn introspection as self-indulgent. We shut our eyes to our own and others' emotions. We adamantly deny psychological problems.

7. We secretly strive for recognition and admiration. Our fundamental attitude is: "Strive at all times to demonstrate your strength and superiority." We view most other people as irresponsible, self-indulgent, lazy, incompetent and imperfect.

8. We resemble a whistling tea kettle with the burner on high. We try to keep all the pressure inside us under wraps. Neverthe-

less, people know how uptight we are because our whistle keeps blowing. Demands for perfection boil up within us. Family members find out that they are usually in hot water.

We need to realize how far such a life-style departs from the biblical principle of resting and trusting in the Lord for every facet of daily living. He doesn't need us to control everything and everyone. He needs us to surrender more often to his spontaneous and mysterious ways of accomplishing his will. "Trust in Lord with all your heart and do not rely on your own insight"(Prov 3:5).

How Controllers Can Move Toward Balance

It may take a divorce, a near fatal car accident, a child gone far astray or a heart attack to force controllers to become aware of the shallowness of this life-style. Such a catastrophe may be a blessing in disguise—a Divine entreaty to slow down, relax and experience spiritual and psychological growth.

In other words, controlling people need to exchange pride for humility. They need to open their hearts, to God and others, in order to feel more at home with themselves. This will ease the pressure to feel superior.

Competition, individuality, and performance reign supreme in our society. American culture taboos weakness and vulnerability, especially for men. We can seldom afford to express such phrases as: "I am unsure," "I feel vulnerable," "I feel hurt," or "I feel helpless." Yet we need to assimilate these expressions to find balance. At times we all feel anxious, scared, helpless and weak.

When we deny or repress a vital part of our real experience, we lose touch with ourselves and with God. We bolster up a facade, or false self, trying to impress others instead of expressing our honest experience. We may mistakenly believe the myth of our ideal selves as self-secure, flawless and capable in all situations. Scripture targets this vanity: "pride goes before destruction" (Prov 16:18).

The maturing Christian learns to experience and talk about the occasional hurts and disappointments of life. A sharp word from a spouse, disappointment over a shattered hope, a painful misunderstanding with a friend—all need to be talked through instead of ignored and met with a stiff upper lip.

By becoming aware of the primary feeling of hurt, we can do something constructive about it.

We can confront the person who wounded us. We can decide that we are too touchy and work on learning how to handle criticism. We can share the hurt with a trusted friend. The most important thing is to get over our disdain of emotions and learn to be warm and spontaneous.

Larry was a bright boy who grew up in an affluent home. His father, a prominent surgeon, had provided his family with a beautiful home, expensive cars and designer clothes. Larry's father earned respect from his church and community. Larry idolized him. Wanting to grow up to be just like his father, Larry studied hard in school. He determined to be at the head of his class, just like his father—and always in control, just like his father.

But Larry rarely saw his father, who would leave for hospital rounds before his family got up and seldom returned before Larry's bedtime. Larry knew his father best from the plaques and achievement awards on his father's den wall. His mother slept late most mornings and often complained about not feeling well.

When Larry was ten, he heard his parents arguing, which they seldom did. Anger tinged his father's voice. His father complained that the house was a complete mess with dishes piled in the sink most of the time. Larry heard his mother defend herself. "I need more help. It's hard raising Larry all by myself. You're never home to see what it's like!" A housekeeper arrived the next day. But Larry's mother remained the same.

One day Larry overheard the housekeeper gossiping on the phone. "This woman's a real lush, I tell you. Larry survived on his own peanut butter and jelly sandwiches for years. I'm surprised he didn't starve before I came." As he listened, a hot humiliation spread through Larry's body and his mind raced. *My mother is a drunk!* he thought. *Who else knows? Does Dad know?*

Larry knew what he had to do. He had to get the housekeeper fired. He had to protect the family's reputation. He had to take charge.

By the time Larry was twelve, he had become adept at taking care of the house. He waited on his mother when she didn't feel well, but made excuses for her behavior when friends came over.

He thought that everything looked normal to outsiders. He made sure the house was clean and orderly. This way his father wouldn't worry either. Larry became a strong child who kept the family together.

Larry completed high school and college with top grades. He followed his father's footsteps and graduated from medical school. He was anxious to move ahead rapidly. But his residency work demanded a lot. He had to give up much of his self-appointed supervision of his mother. Months went by without contact from his father.

He volunteered for extra hours beyond the impossibly long shifts of his regular assignments. Larry didn't want to miss anything that might keep him ahead of the pack. He viewed himself as far superior to his fellows. In fact, he thought he could teach most of the doctors a thing or two.

Larry was lucky. When his over-confidence and exhaustion caused him to miscalculate a dosage on a patient's prescription, a young nurse named Jennie caught his error in time. But he responded with anger—anger at himself for his mistake, and resentment toward her for pointing it out.

Jennie was impressed by his dedication. At the same time she was sure that another disaster was waiting to happen. In helping him, she felt a bond between them begin to grow. She knew he had been watching her too. But now his watching had taken on a new character. He was surly and demanding, checking up on her work and looking for mistakes he seemed sure she was making.

She finally confronted him with her frustration. "You've been on my back for weeks now, and I know I don't deserve it."

Larry relented after more arguing, and apologized to her. He explained how important his medical career was to him.

Jennie told him that she admired his expertise and commitment. Larry needed to hear that from her badly. He confided all his dreams and plans to her. She seemed as interested in them as he was.

They saw each other regularly. Within a few months, he asked her to marry him. Then their conflicts began all over again. She wanted to continue her career so they could work together. He wanted her to quit even before they were married.

"It costs money to start a medical practice. We need my income," Jennie argued.

"Your income is nothing," Larry shouted. "I don't need your income. It wouldn't even keep us in toothpaste! Besides, wives of professional men don't work. It's demeaning."

"I'm a professional too," Jennie responded with hurt in her voice.

"I can take care of my career," said Larry, "and I can take care of my money. I want my wife to take care of herself."

Larry yearned to marry Jennie, but she resisted his carefully laid plans for his life. The harder he tried to make her understand, the more stubborn she became. He faced difficulties with his career too, but he couldn't share them with her. He was sure he would lose her if he told her he was having trouble getting a large enough loan to start his practice.

Larry visited his mother one afternoon, and found himself confessing all his problems to her. This was quite a role reversal. He had spent years protecting her, and now he was parading all his fears in front of this weak, pathetic woman.

"I've been thinking about how much responsibility you've had to carry all alone since you were a young child," said his mother. "I feel sorry about it. I want you to know how much I care for you and appreciate your strength. I want to do something for you now, but I have to have your promise that you'll accept it before I tell you what it is."

With much puzzlement and some protest, Larry finally promised. To his astonishment, she stated: "I want you to join a therapy group. I'll pay. I think it's time you found out that others have something to offer."

Transformation at Last

Larry was very willing to talk when he first joined my therapy group. He explained that he was only there to please his mother. He dazzled the group with stories about medicine, with himself in the starring role.

One of the group members asked, "Do bad things ever happen even when you're strong?" Thoughts of Jennie rushed into Larry's head. He shifted in his chair and stared down at the carpet.

"When you're strong, you can control things, have them your way," Larry responded.

"What about people? Can you always control people?" I asked.

"If you're strong enough, I suppose you can," he mumbled.

I had an idea. "Larry, would you be willing to try a little experiment with the group? It has to do with strength and weakness. I think we might all find it valuable."

"That depends," he hesitated.

"It's simple," I said. "You're a strong man physically. All you have to do is lie on the floor. Four of us will position ourselves by your arms and legs to try and hold you down. You try to get up. I want you to find out if strength can always control things, and if it can't, what it feels like to be helpless."

Larry smiled broadly. "Oh, is that all? I'm strong. I don't think just four of you can hold me down."

"That's fine," I said. "I want you to know that this is just an exercise, though. If you want to stop, let us know and we will."

"Got it," Larry said with the same smile.

After Larry lay down on the carpet, the four volunteers positioned themselves at each arm and leg. "All right, Larry, get up," I ordered.

Larry strained with all his might and his face turned red. But the group members exerted equal pressure downward and held him firm. After a minute or so, he relaxed to catch his breath.

Then he squirmed and twisted with full strength to raise himself up again, but was unable to budge. He repeated this pattern several more times.

Christ made no effort to conceal his own feelings of weakness and vulnerability.

Now Larry wasn't laughing. With a surge of desperation, he tried to buck them off. His arms and legs trembled and he gasped for breath. He had overestimated his strength. He looked scared and ashamed.

Suddenly, he began to cry, quietly at first, then in huge deep sobs that seemed to rumble from way down inside him. I told the group to let him up, and they helped him to his feet.

Larry sat down and began to talk about what he had just learned.

"I was thinking of my fiancee," he said. "I think she's been trying to tell me for a long time that I need to back off and quit trying so hard. I've been trying to control her and to be strong for her. It almost broke us up. I've been hitting a lot of brick walls lately." His eyes teared again, and he said, this time with a relaxed smile, "I think I got the message. I have a peaceful feeling inside. I can't wait to see Jennie!"

So began Larry's journey toward a balanced personality.

For a controlling person to begin moving to the opposite polarity of weakness, the first step is to recognize and own vulnerable feelings when they occur. A good person to model is Jesus.

Christ made no effort to conceal his own occasional feelings of weakness and vulnerability. The Gospel relates that in a memorable moment before Jesus called forth Lazarus from the tomb: "Jesus wept" (Jn 11:35). The biblical writer chose a Greek expression which means *cried with real tears*. It differentiated the sincere sadness welling up in Jesus' heart from ritualistic mourning.

Christ was secure enough in himself to freely experience the rhythm between strength and weakness, with no inner sense of shame or apology.

Another poignant moment occurred in the Garden of Gethsemane when Jesus singled out Peter, James, and John—his closest disciples—and asked them to sustain him in his hour of greatest pain and soul-searching. Profoundly aware of his weakness, he said to them, "My soul is exceedingly sorrowful unto death...and he went forward a little, and fell on the ground, and prayed that, if it were possible, the hour might pass from him" (Mk 14:34-35).

A fellow psychologist who is in his sixties attended one of my workshops and discovered that he had been a controlling perfectionist for years. He wrote in a letter:

> Throughout my childhood my mother referred to me as "Mom's little soldier." She and my father had certain difficulties in their relationship, and somehow she unconsciously put the burden of responsible behavior onto me. I never really had a childhood where I could romp and laugh and play.
>
> Recently in the workshop you asked each of us to state our most important goal in life. I said that mine had been to be an eagle on top of a mountain peak, a leader at the pinnacle of my profession. As I spoke, I suddenly realized how empty I felt inside. At the break, a woman came up and said she felt sad for me—she sensed that I was a very lonely man. I denied it at first, but then tears came to my eyes. I think it was the first time I've ever cried as an adult.
>
> When we returned to the session, you asked us to role-play an opposite experience to our conscious goal in life. You called this a growth stretch into our most feared polarity. For

me, it was becoming a little boy again and putting my head in the lap of that woman who saw my loneliness. I trusted her. For a few moments she became the warm and accepting mother I never had.

As a youngster I always had to perform and keep my feelings inside. But as this sensitive woman caressed my hair and told me that it was okay to cry, I suddenly felt loved for being myself. I will never forget the feeling. I felt free from the burden of trying to convince everyone how strong I am.

Much to our surprise, we will find that confessing our faults and expressing our needs causes people to respect us more, not less. To be fully human, accepting both strengths and weaknesses, opens the door to intimacy and acceptance. It leads off the treadmill of futile perfectionism and onto the path of a balanced personality.

In confessing our weaknesses, we give up our pretense of being larger than life. We let go of our Rock of Gibraltar complexes and give others, including God, the opportunity to bless us with their empathy, their support and their love.

"No man is an island," wrote John Donne. The sharing of our deepest anxieties, doubts and fears enables us to experience the joy of being alone no more.

PRACTICAL GROWTH STEPS

1. Give up your need to impress others. Relax. Live and let live. Do less, and enjoy it more. Practice laughing at your mistakes this week, and let your schedule slide if it means helping someone else.

2. Challenge your own attitudes of superiority when they manifest themselves. Practice spreading compliments, praise and joy about others' accomplishments this week. Realize that someone else's success does not diminish you.

3. Ask for more perceptual feedback from friends and loved ones this week. How do you really see me? Am I compulsive to a

fault? Would you like me better if I didn't pretend to know everything? Is it true that I'm tense, grim and nit-picky? When they give you an honest answer, thank them for their personal candor and tell them you want to become more playful and loving.

4. Do three things that are frivolous, silly and spontaneous this week. Go ride on a park swing, give someone an African violet, give your spouse a massage, buy a family game and make some popcorn, buy a non-traditional outfit, go to lunch with the gang, take a day off and snooze or watch videos. Realize that the best contributions you can make have to do with being warm, spontaneous and accepting of people's differences.

5. Ask the Holy Spirit to reveal and heal your tendencies toward the controlling perspective. Write in your prayer diary the insights about your personality that you gain from the following scriptures:

Zechariah 4:6—*Not by might, nor by power, but by my spirit, says the Lord of hosts.*

2 Corinthians 12:9—*My grace is sufficient for you: for my power is made perfect in weakness.*

Romans 14:10—*Why do you pass judgment on your brother? Or you, why do you despise your brother? For we shall all stand before the judgment seat of God.*

Luke 6:41-42—*Why do you see the speck that is in your brother's eye, but do not notice the log that is in your own eye? Or how can you say to your brother, "Brother, let me take out the speck that is in your eye," when you yourself do not see the log that is in your own eye? You hypocrite, first take the log out of your own eye, and then you will see clearly to take out the speck that is in your brother's eye.*

Isaiah 57:15—*For thus says the high and lofty One who inhabits eternity, whose name is Holy; I dwell in the high and holy place, and also with him who is of a contrite and humble spirit, to revive the spirit of the humble, and to revive the heart of the contrite.*

Romans 12:16—*Live in harmony with one another; do not be haughty, but associate with the lowly; never be conceited.*

Isaiah 5:21—*Woe to those who are wise in their own eyes, and shrewd in their own sight!*

James 4:6—*God opposes the proud, but gives grace to the humble.*

Eight

Beyond Manipulation

IN MY EARLY TWENTIES, WHILE TEACHING Ethics in a college, I gave a lecture on spiritual love. The students took notes voraciously and one young woman told me the lecture moved her deeply. Yet I came away from the class knowing my own behavior was far from Christlike. I was becoming aware of problems in my personality that were distorting my ability to give and receive love.

When I craved attention, I found a way to show off. When I wanted someone to like me, I tried to impress them with my accomplishments. When I felt hurt, I hid my pain under a mask of sullen detachment. When I felt resentful, I put on a frozen smile to hide my anger, yet still harbored a grudge. These manipulative behaviors blocked my ability to interact honestly with people.

I felt powerless to change my manipulative ways. That night I begged the Lord for help. I prayed, "Father, help me quit living in my mind and start feeling with my heart. Help me to stop puffing myself up, withdrawing when I don't get my way and holding anger inside. Please help me love others and myself like you do."

Before long, the still, small voice of the Lord spoke within me:

> Dan, you have done well in loving and serving me, but you're still afraid of people. You're afraid they won't respect you if you don't show strength. You're afraid they will reject

> you if you reveal weaknesses. You're afraid they will hurt you if you open your heart to love. You're afraid they'll disapprove if you express your feelings.
>
> But I love people, even though some of them reject, hurt and hate me. Are you willing to be more of your real self and take the risks of love?

Wasn't that the crux of the matter? God was showing me that my intellectual pride and emotional defensiveness had boxed me into a corner. I wanted love without being vulnerable. I needed to be strong without being weak, to be in control without risking my heart. This inner revelation gave me new hope. Without realizing it, I was being tutored in the LAWS of personality and relationships. That night I invited the Holy Spirit to give me the courage to love.

Each of us is partly manipulative and partly capable of Christlike love. Though boxed in by our fears, pride and defensiveness, we can risk being more of our real selves and learn to love beyond manipulation.

You now understand how partial personality perspectives can thwart a person's God-inspired impulses toward wholeness. You know how they can block authentic responses to others through love, assertiveness, weakness and strength. When we overlook or ignore the LAWS of personality, our behavior deteriorates into manipulation. The good news is that we can reverse manipulation by using our compass of the self and trusting the Holy Spirit in our core.

Manipulation is defined as treating other people as things—exploiting, using and controlling them in ways that destroy spiritual love. The way of Christ is not achieved by fear, guilt or coercion, but by love. The way of Christ invites us to:

- appreciate others as persons
- understand ourselves
- participate in a loving community
- mature beyond manipulation

Top Dogs and Underdogs

Most of us manipulate others in one of two ways: either as top dogs who use the strength and assertion poles to control people, or as underdogs who use the love and weakness poles to make others take responsibility for us. Uncertain that we are acceptable the way we are, we don the mask of the manipulator.

In Christian culture, men tend to adopt top dog patterns of manipulation—being competitive, arrogant and dictatorial. In a radio interview, a man called in to attack me for stating that men need to develop their capacity for tenderness, humility and affection.

"You just want to turn us into a bunch of sissies," he said. "Men are supposed to be strong so they can take care of their women!"

"I am suggesting that men will be better lovers and fathers if we take the chip off our shoulders," I replied. "We need to learn to say 'I'm sorry' when we're wrong, and offer more hugs and 'I love yous' to our families."

The caller hung up on me.

On the other hand, the underdog patterns of being codependent, naive and needing constant reassurance trap many women. I once appeared for an interview on a Christian women's program that satellite television beamed out to millions. The hostess asked me to describe what would be a detrimental personality style for women. I replied that the worst thing a woman could do was to be submissive, dependent and unaware of her own capabilities. The hostess' mouth dropped open and her hand went to her lips. "Dr. Montgomery," she exclaimed, "you just described 90% of the women who watch this program!"

Unfortunately, little boys are still socialized into top dog styles when their elders discourage them from expressing tender or vulnerable feelings. Adults still train little girls to be submissive and sweet. When my wife and I direct parental workshops, we teach the compass model to parents so they can encourage their boys and girls to develop balanced personalities.

As a parent, you may spot tendencies in your child to get stuck in just one compass point, becoming aggressive, submissive, withdrawn or bossy. You can encourage creative growth stretches into the other compass points until balance is gradually achieved.

Once we have opened our deepest selves to Christ, human nature is no longer an enemy but a friend. Self-acceptance comes when we surrender our whole self to God.

In relationships between men and women, men generally need to develop more humility, vulnerability, affection and nurturance. Women usually need to work on more objectivity, assertion, confidence and identity. Both sexes gradually develop more whole and fully-functioning personalities. This dramatically enhances communication between the sexes.

As Father Powell writes: "We hear people say resignedly, 'This is the way I am....' They do not seem to acknowledge the hope-filled truth that we can break old and crippling habits of perception and cultivate new, life-giving habits."[18]

Expanding Your Personality

The new, life-giving habits of the LAWS and the Holy Spirit in our core help us distinguish between authenticity and manipulation. The following diagram is a tool which distinguishes between core-inspired self expression and fear-driven manipulation.

The compass of the self includes both negative and positive aspects of our behavior. The innermost ring represents the major manipulative tactics we employ when stuck on a particular compass point. We usually act out these self-defeating behaviors without

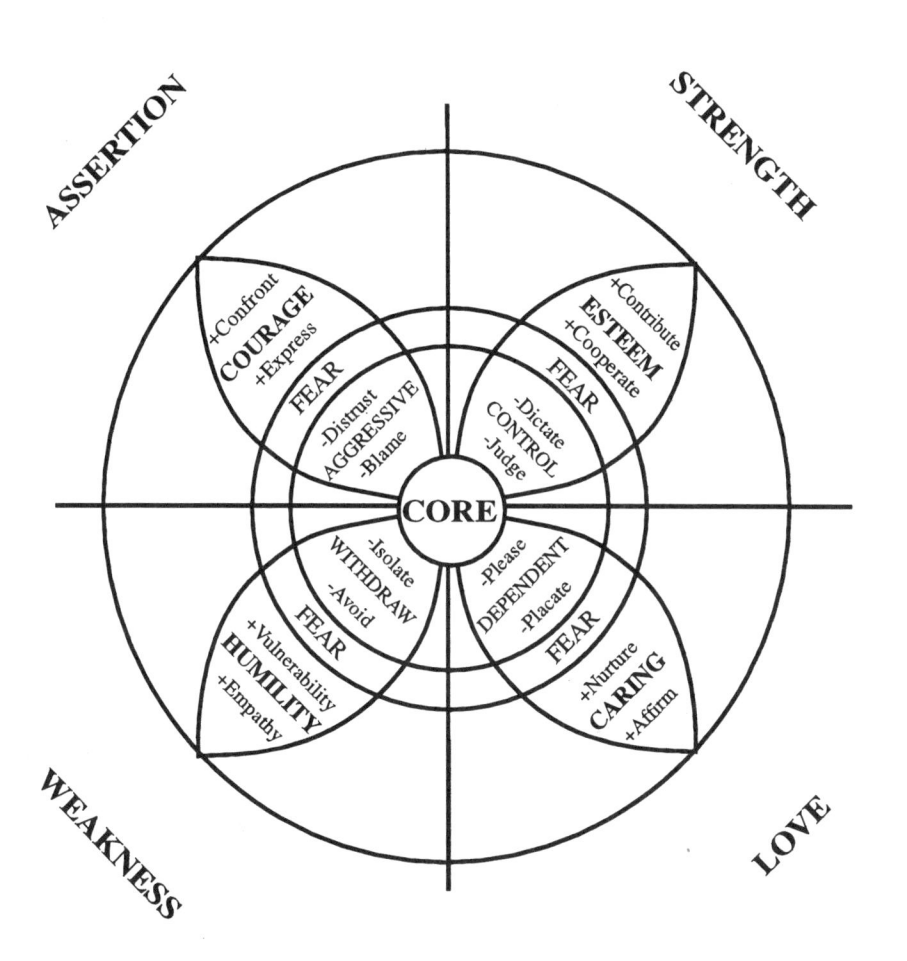

EXPANDING THE PERSONALITY

knowing it. The "Ring of Fear" can constrict our core and block the flow of the Holy Spirit.

When we recognize that we are stuck in a manipulative pattern (inner circle of diagram), we also see how to stretch into authentic self-expression (outer circle of diagram). Utilizing the diagram, we see how the authentic expression of all four compass points adds up to a whole self—a balanced personality.

On the love polarity, we can transform pleasing and placating into nurturing and affirming. These qualities yield the *virtue of caring*, a sure mark of the maturing Christian. On the assertion polarity, we can re-shape distrusting and blaming into expressing and confronting. The person who expresses assertion in diplomatic ways exhibits the *virtue of courage*. On the weakness polarity, we can change isolating and avoiding into empathy and vulnerability. These traits form the *virtue of humility*. On the strength polarity, we can transfigure dictating and judging into cooperating and contributing. These traits give birth to the *virtue of esteem*.

As you can see, real wisdom is built into the warp and woof of human nature. Once we have opened our deepest selves to Christ, human nature is no longer an enemy but a friend. Self-acceptance comes when we surrender our whole self to God. A dynamic rhythm that draws equally from all four compass points releases the artesian flow of the Spirit. Jesus fills our personalities with himself.

Any act can express either relating or manipulating. We can smile out of joy in seeing you, or we can smile to make it look that way. We can cry as a result of genuine sorrow for you, or we can cry to make you feel guilty. Expression wells up as an unrehearsed outpouring. Manipulation calculates and demands a response. Expression is a fountain; manipulation is a whirlpool. With expression we feel emotionally touched; with manipulation we feel sucked in and drained. With manipulation life is a wrestling match. With expression, life is a dance.

Gayle Erwin writes, in *The Jesus Style*:

> A particular characteristic of manipulation is that it destroys our ability to choose. It forces us to move defensively into the pattern or mold that others have chosen for us. Not a single person who tried to manipulate Jesus got the answer they expected. All of them received an expression of the true feelings of Jesus. From some of them he withdrew. In each case he protected his ability to choose.
>
> There is a distinctive difference between coerced slavery and servanthood by choice. When Jesus stated that he chose to lay down his life and that no one was taking it from him, he was describing the basic element of love.... True love cannot be the result of either decree, force or manipulation. Anything that I do to deprive someone of the right to choose is a violation of his personhood. When I sense that my own right to choose is being threatened, then I know that I am not being loved.[19]

Studying this diagram can help to free you from someone else's attempts to manipulate you. For instance, if you recognize that a friend is in the habit of clinging to you, constantly asking for reassurance and advice, yet never getting any better, you can distance yourself enough for your friend to stand on his or her own feet. Or if a boss or co-worker often intimidates you by blaming and attacking, you can confront them and explain that you will not allow them to scapegoat you. You can:

- say you would like them to work at not getting your attention in negative ways
- quit trying to win their approval
- work on building and keeping positive self-esteem in spite of their attitudes
- confront them each time they attempt to criticize you
- use humor to counteract their barbs or jibes

The change from manipulation to authenticity promotes personality transformation. Manipulative deception becomes transparent honesty. Deadness turns into aliveness. The freedom to live spontaneously from the heart replaces the need to control or be controlled. By the grace of God, cynicism turns into hope-filled faith. The following chart illustrates the transformation process.

MANIPULATION	*AUTHENTICITY*
1. *Deception* (Phoniness, Hidden Agendas, Duplicity): The use of gimmicks, games, and maneuvers. Putting on a front, playing a role to create an impression. "Putting on" feelings.	1. *Honesty* (Transparency, Genuineness, Authenticity): The ability to express feelings openly, rather than repress or falsify them. The use of candor and sincerity. The ability to speak from the heart.
2. *Unawareness* (Deadness, Superficiality, Boredom): Having tunnel vision. Hearing and seeing only what one wishes. Captive to own rigid biases. Being a top dog or underdog.	2. *Awareness* (Responsivity, Aliveness, Interest): Listening deeply to self and others. Open to new information, insight, and discoveries. Vital involvement in life and personal growth.
3. *Control* (Closed-minded, Deliberate, Calculating): Playing life like a chess game. Needing to control or be controlled. Concealing motives from other. Needing sameness. Fighting change and growth.	3. *Freedom* (Spontaneity, Openness, Creativity): An adventurer in life. Allowing for novelty, change and growth. A sense of autonomy, responsibility and grace. Expressing all the polarities of personality.
4. *Cynicism* (Distrust, Skepticism): Being basically distrustful of self and others. Deep down a fear of being natural, a fear of accepting life without ploys and magical thinking. Seeing only two options to relationships—control or be controlled.	4. *Trust* (Faith, Sensitivity): An abiding trust in the love and grace of God. Accepting both one's good traits and personality defects. Forgiving self and others. Preferring dialogue and intimacy to manipulation and control.

EXERCISES

1. Take out a sheet of paper and draw a large circle in the middle. Now slice this "pie" into four pieces, which represent proportionately how often you express the virtues revealed in the LAWS—caring, courage, humility and esteem.

Which slice is the smallest? Think of ways to make that slice of energy more equal to the rest. Which slice is the largest? Could this represent an over-reliance on one of the polarities and a neglect of the others? How do you want your energy pie to look in the future?

2. Spend some time in thought and prayer about one relationship in which you currently feel confused and manipulated. Figure out where the other person fits into the diagram titled "Expanding the Personality." Discover which compass point you've been stuck on in reacting to him or her. You are free to grow and change. Since that person's behavior is predictable, you need fear it no more. Ask the Holy Spirit to help you actively change your responses to this person.

3. Write on a sheet of paper all the ways in which you manipulate people. Then write in big, bold letters the word *fear* across the page. Now, if you are willing to give up the masks of manipulation, crumple the paper in your fist. Throw the paper in the wastebasket. Feel your determination to let go of the control you have tried to master, and just be yourself more and more with people. Feel the power of the Holy Spirit setting you free from fear, pride and manipulation.

Ask God to be with you in a real way today—to heal your fears, inspire your creativity, and fill your spiritual core.

Nine

Techniques for Transformation

A FRIEND OF MINE NAMED MIGUEL IS a famous potter. This bearded, Catholic Cuban has one of his pots displayed in the Smithsonian. One day I watched him mold a brand new pot out of muddy red clay. He took a huge piece of the clay, massaged it with skillful hands, added water to it and plopped it down on the potter's wheel. At first the clay was tough and unyielding. But as he continued to knead it with his strong yet gentle hands, the clay became more supple. I could see that Miguel loved the pot he was forming. He whistled while he worked, and he smiled as the clay responded to him.

When he was about an hour into his work on this particular pot, I began to notice that while it had taken shape nicely, there were still many imperfections on its sides—lumps and jagged edges. These bothered me, but didn't disturb Miguel. He kept whistling and smiling. Suddenly, with a movement so deft I hardly saw it, he cut off the lumps and smoothed the ridges. He looked up at me, sweat pouring from his forehead and announced with joy, "Done!" He set it aside for baking in the kiln that night.

A few days later he gave me that pot. He had decorated it with golden highlights to accentuate its maroon color. Tears welled up in my eyes. I marveled at how Miguel had crafted something so beautiful out of mud. I take Miguel's pot with me to conferences where I describe how God does the work of patiently sculpting our personalities. Our part is to remain supple and yielding so that God can transform our whole being—conscious and unconscious—into a unique and eternal expression of Christ.

The Courage of Imperfection

Thomas Merton writes: "One of the most important aspects of any religious vocation...is the willingness to accept life in a community in which everybody is more or less imperfect."[20] I call this the *courage of imperfection*. For Jesus reveals the descent of God to our lives, just as we are, not the ascent of our lives to God, hoping he might approve when he sees how hard we try.

Personality transformation occurs through grace, a kind of effortless effort; not by striving to please God or obey all the rules. Jesus, the Master Potter, said it this way:

> Get away with me and you'll recover your life. I'll show you how to take a real rest. Walk with me and work with me—watch how I do it. Learn the unforced rhythms of grace. I won't lay anything heavy or ill-fitting on you. Keep company with me and you'll learn to live freely and lightly (Mt 11:28-30).[21]

How is it possible that the perfect love of God can heal our fear, defensiveness and pride? It happens because the growing Christian learns to live in an atmosphere of *inspiration* rather than condemnation. The love and power of God through Christ perfect our personality and the Holy Spirit works to transform our core.

According to *Webster's*, to perfect means "to bring to final form." As we actively trust the Lord for support and growth in every aspect of being, he will heal our fears and personality rigidities. We never arrive at complete perfection this side of heaven. Our testimony isn't that we are perfect, but that we have met the Redeemer.

We needn't live in fear that we'll make a mistake or fall short of perfection. Christ died for our mistakes and shortcomings, so the battle of righteousness versus sin is over. With Christ living within us, we need not live in a spirit of fear. As John says, "There is no fear in love; but perfect love casts out fear" (1 Jn 4:18). We remain imperfect, but God's perfect love now lives within us and slowly transforms us.

Bringing Together Our Outer and Inner Selves

"How can I live a fuller Christian life?" ask many Catholics. One of my favorite techniques for assisting people to get closer to themselves and to God is the *art box.* I describe this self-help technique more fully in my book, *How to Survive Practically Anything.*[22] Many priests, religious and spiritual directors use the art box to encourage spiritual and personality growth. People construct art boxes in church classes or on their own. The art box is a great communication tool between married couples.

Here's how to make an art box:

- Select a box of any size and shape to symbolize your personality. You can use a shoe box, hat box, gift box, grocery box—whatever seems right.

- Start collecting pictures, images, words, poems, or objects that represent different aspects of your life and self-image. These can be collected from magazines, family scrapbooks, postcards or memorabilia—or specially created.

- The outside of the box represents your "public self." On the outside, make a collage showing how you present yourself to others, to the world and to God. Take your time, be curious and enjoy the process.

- When you complete the outside of the art box, shift to what goes inside this box. This represents your "private self"—

your innermost thoughts, secrets, desires, needs, feelings, hurts and dreams.
- Take one week to complete the project and plan to share it for about half an hour.
- Choose a person or group where confidentiality is assured.

Here are the guidelines for sharing your box. Set up a special time to share your art box with a growth group, a trusted friend or your family. Say that you are seeking to gain insight into your life and personality. It is by sharing the intimate details of your box with God and other people that you are made more whole. Take your time while disclosing what each part of the box means to you. Assume the attitude that anything human is worthy of understanding.

Explore your emotions. Do parts of the box make you happy, sad, vulnerable or proud? Say so. Be curious about what makes you tick. It's okay for your strengths and weaknesses to show through.

If another person shares his or her art box with you, show interest in every aspect of their sharing, without passing any judgment. People gain the most from their art boxes in a warm interpersonal climate of trust.

A forty-five-year old businessman named Brandon pasted images from *Time and Fortune* magazines onto the outside of his art box. The pictures depicted financial and business success: a wad of money; a three-story Victorian home; a computer work station and the phrase: "Numero Uno." The black and white shades of the art box matched Brandon's personality—grim and serious.

"I keep thinking that if I can just put one more dollar in the bank, I'll be happy," he said, as we examined his box. But the empty inside of the box troubled him.

"I thought this project was a snap until I looked for something to go inside the box," he said. "I can't come up with anything. I started to paste more pictures like those on the outside, but it didn't feel right. I don't really know what's inside me!"

"What about your relationships?" I queried. "You have a daughter and a wife. Where are they in your life?"

"I don't think about them very much. I'm too busy with my work."

"What about friends, God and humanity? Do you love anyone?"

These questions haunted Brandon. The honest answer we came up with was that he based his life on achievements, not relationships—on business, not intimacy. This accounted for depression and anxiety even in the face of financial success.

I encouraged Brandon to reevaluate his goals in life—to do what I call a *priority recital.* If he persisted in being an emotionally absent spouse and parent, Brandon could eventually lose the love of his family.

During the next session, I complimented Brandon for his industry and hard work, but wondered if he ever felt like the world rested on his shoulders. I expressed admiration for his financial competencies, but asked if he missed the warmth of love. A glint of tears moistened his eyes.

"I've built my own little castle of selfishness," he whispered. "I don't let Sharon, my daughter, or anyone else inside. This is the same way my father lived and I'm sick of it! Is it too late to change?"

"Brandon," I said, "you're changing right now. Your tears are watering your soul. Growth is going to follow!"

I suggested that he seek less to impress people with his business acumen and start becoming more human.

"What will people think?" he asked, eyebrows raised.

"They'll think you're more likable," I assured him.

We prayed together and I didn't see him for the next four months.

One day Brandon walked back into my office grinning like a Cheshire cat. He wore Levi's instead of his usual three-piece suit. He handed me a newly revised version of the art box. I was intrigued, as I didn't remember Brandon ever smiling before.

One of the old business pictures remained on the outside of his new box. The other pictures included a family in the park; a man and a woman sailing together in a skiff; a daddy and a daughter eating popcorn at the zoo; three children giggling as they released some brightly colored balloons into the blue sky; and a man in his office with a smile on his face. Brandon's powers for play, humor and love had come of age.

In kindergarten-style handwriting around the inside of the box were the words, *"living, learning and loving."* Every letter in the motto was printed in a different color crayon. I was fascinated by the object inside his box: a red helium-filled balloon which contained folded strips of paper.

I asked Brandon what these stood for. He said the five folded pieces of paper inside the balloon read: "compulsive," "tense," "serious," "controlling," and "insensitive."

Brandon took the red balloon out of the box and asked me to walk outside my office with him. As we stood there surrounded by pine trees, he smiled broadly and then let the balloon go. The helium balloon soared upward against the backdrop of a cobalt sky and puffs of white clouds. We watched for several minutes until the balloon became a little red dot. Then it disappeared.

The art box helps us understand what makes us tick. With the benefit of awareness and healing prayer, we can surrender more fully to the Lord. Give it a try.

Handling Guilt

Many people falter in spiritual growth because they feel guilt about something that happened in the past. But guilt exists in a sacred polarity with its opposite: grace. Any guilt we feel is always a pathway to confession and restoration of our identity in God.

Nothing can liberate us more than coming clean with past sins of omission or commission, and confessing them to another person and to God. The power of the confessional gives us a frequent fresh experience of absolution and grace. But sometimes we need to face our wrongdoing by speaking directly to those we've harmed and by making amends. God is always with us when we do this, even though we may feel anxious at the time.

Guilt is a tormenting feeling. But we can choose how long we are willing to put up with it.

Recently I made an amends for a wrong I committed thirty years ago. I mentioned in the first chapter that I was raised in a tough town and came to be violent myself. I spoke about how I beat up my best friend, Lewis. After I came to know Christ at the age of seventeen, I made amends to all of the people I'd threatened or harmed except one, Lewis. I just felt too embarrassed to face him. I figured that he hated my guts and that he could never forgive me. I rationalized that I should let sleeping dogs lie.

So I repressed my guilt. I sent it underground so I wouldn't think about it. However my unconscious reminded me of this unhealed wound for the next thirty years. I had regular nightmares about Lewis rejecting me, taunting me and accusing me. Inside my personality, God was prompting me to come clean with Lewis.

This year I wrote a magazine article about confessing our sins and making amends. One afternoon while finishing the piece, the gentle voice of the Holy Spirit spoke within me. "What about Lewis, Dan?" he said. "Why don't you contact him and ask for his forgiveness?"

I shuddered. *I don't know where he lives,* I thought, *and besides, he hates my guts and would never want to hear from me.* About an hour later my phone rang. My mother said, "Danny, guess what? Your old friend Lewis just moved to Santa Fe. Why don't you ask him out for lunch?" This confirmed that now was the time to make amends. Yet I felt the stabbing pain of anxiety in my stomach.

I asked the Lord to give me courage to face my fears and I called Lewis. When he recognized my voice, he said in a gruff tone, "What do you want?" I invited him to lunch the next day.

I was seated at a booth when Lewis arrived, scowling. I kept praying under my breath for the Holy Spirit to encompass us. When Lewis sat down across from me, I came straight to the point. "Lewis, do you remember how I came after you in high school and attacked you?"

"Of course I do," he replied.

"Well, I want you to know that I've felt guilt all these years. It was a terrible, stupid thing to do." Tears welled up and my heart pounded. "I am so sorry. I was filled with hate in those days and I let it out at you. Is there any way you can forgive me?" I handed him a Hallmark card that spoke of friendship.

He opened the card and read what I had to say. He looked up at me and took a deep breath. "I forgive you, Danny," he said, a smile breaking across his face. "I don't hold it against you." He reached across the table and we shook hands. Peace streamed throughout my body. My heart jumped for joy. We spent the next hour catching up on those thirty years. When we left the restaurant, we exchanged bear hugs.

If there's a confession waiting in your unconscious for the moment of truth, bring the situation into full awareness. Guilt is a tormenting feeling. But we can choose how long we are willing to put up with it. To get guilt off our chests, we ask God for forgiveness and make amends as best we can. This process transforms negative emotional conflicts into positive growth and joy.

Experiencing Spiritual Support

In one of my Prayer and Personal Growth Seminars, I found that many of the participants believed in Christ and the Holy Spirit, but had difficulty experiencing the love of God in their bodies. A woman named Patricia said she had tried unsuccessfully to give her worries to the Lord. Despite an active prayer life, she seemed to face one crisis after another. The current ordeal was coping with her daughter's wedding the following Saturday.

As Patty described her anxiety over the wedding preparations, I noticed her body speaking volumes. Her shoulders were raised two inches higher than normal. Her brow was furrowed and lips tightly pursed. I invited Patty to try an experiment.

I asked seven people from the group to stand behind her, hands outstretched, to form a "hammock" for her to lie in. "Patty, this hammock of hands symbolizes the peace available from the Holy Spirit," I said. "I'd like you to lean back a little at a time until your feet leave the floor. The group will completely support you."

"But what if they drop me?" she gulped.

"That's just the point," I explained. "Your body is so uptight that you don't trust anyone, including God. This exercise gives you a chance to let go and let God."

"Well, I don't think this is going to help," she argued.

Patty began to lean into the caring hands pressed gently against her back and legs. Suddenly, she jerked back up. "I can't go through with this!" she exclaimed. "I feel nervous. I *know* they'll drop me!"

"That is your biggest problem with God and people," I said. "You pray to God but your body resists him. You tell your problems to people, but never trust their support. Now try again." I offered a prayer to help her, "Holy Spirit, help Patty surrender all her worries to you. She's going to trust you completely. Please bring your peace and comfort into her body."

Patty heaved a sigh as she leaned back into the human hammock. Within moments she was floating on an air mattress of caring support. She lay there several minutes. Her shoulders began to melt and her breathing deepened. Her body loosened like a handful of rubber bands. "How are you feeling?" I asked.

"This feels great," she said. "Can I stay here for awhile?"

"Yes," I replied. The group gently rocked her. Patty breathed from her belly. A smile peeped around the corners of her mouth. "Now pretend it's the day *after* your daughter's the wedding," I suggested. "You're relaxed and your body feels the way it does right now. You remember how the Holy Spirit helped you out." Patty's face radiated bliss. "You've trusted God and those around you," I continued. "The wedding was peaceful and filled with love."

Depression is often the other side of the coin of buried resentment.

Patty opened her eyes. "Is this what it feels like to trust God?" she whispered.

"Yes, this is how we feel when our bodies rest in the Holy Spirit," I replied. "Let your body remember all you've learned today."

The group eased Patty back into a standing position. Tears flowed down her cheeks. "I'm feeling joy," she said and then hugged every one of us.

The next week Patty told us that the wedding had gone beautifully. Family and friends had commented that she didn't fuss or fume. "I just really let go and trusted God," she said. "I didn't feel like I had to be Mrs. Perfect and control everything. Whenever I would start to tense up, I remembered the Holy Spirit hammock and my body relaxed. I enjoyed the preparations and the wedding too!"

Facing Our Deepest Feelings

A college student named Anne suffered from a depression that she could neither explain nor rise above. Depression is often the other side of the coin of buried resentment. While talking to her, I kept listening with my third ear for a clue to indicate with whom she felt angry.

As the last child in a family of nine children, Anne reflected, "I'm like the runt of the litter. Everybody always ignored me—especially my mother. She was always too busy to give me any attention."

When Anne described her childhood family environment, I could tell that her mother was not the angry or abusive sort, but rather a sensitive soul who was simply overwhelmed and worn out from raising so many children. In this kind of situation, it is best to encourage people to speak directly to the person with whom they are angry.

Surprisingly, many people have never thought of directly sharing their hurt or anger. But a sincere effort to get anger off our chests often clears the air of phoniness and improves the quality of the relationship.

When I suggested to Anne that she use her next weekend at home to openly discuss her longtime resentments toward her mother, she exclaimed, "I can't do that. We don't talk about feelings in our home."

"Now is a good time to start," I suggested. "You may be the first one to break the emotional barrier and come clean with your real feelings. Why don't you give it a try?"

The next weekend Anne returned home and sought a way to face her deepest feelings. She brought her journal to our next session and read aloud the following entry:

> I was mad. Mad at life, people, and God. Mainly I felt mad at myself. The anger swept over me like a tornado as I drove home from our therapy session.
>
> I wanted the intimacy you talked about. But all I had inside was this anger. The little girl inside of me built a wall around her a long time ago to hide her pain and sorrow. That

little girl would deny that bad feelings existed. She would smile at everybody while hating life.

My whole way of life suddenly seemed like a stage in which I played a part but never truly expressed my feelings. I never experienced honesty and openness. What would that be like? I didn't even know why I felt so angry.

I arrived home and everything started off wrong. My mom and I started our usual pattern of bickering back and forth. The anger kept building up but I couldn't express it openly. I thought to myself, *why won't she let me get rid of this anger?*

I left the house and walked to the top of the hill. Yet even alone with nature I couldn't find a release. *Nobody will let me get this anger out!* I thought.

Then it hit me: I wouldn't let myself get rid of the anger. It didn't belong to anyone else. It was me who was holding the anger inside. I could no longer blame other people or God. I had to take responsibility for my emotions. I went back to the house still feeling angry, but confused as to how to express it. We just didn't express anger directly in our home.

The next morning I woke up with the same angry feelings. I felt like I was going to burst if something didn't happen. Later that morning I was standing by the heater when Mom said something to me. The dam inside me burst and a flood of resentful feelings came out.

I started crying and yelling at my mom, "Ever since I was a child I've never felt like you loved me. You never had time for me. You were always listening to my brothers and sisters! I was a little girl in a big confusing world with all these big people. Nobody took time for me! Not you or anyone else!"

Mom started crying and yelling back, "I did my best. What else could I do?" Then she ran out of the house.

I dropped on the floor sobbing. I thought to myself, *Here*

we go again. Another time I need you and you walk out on me. All I want you to do is show me love, but you leave me instead. I lay there crying my eyes out.

Then Mom came back into the house. I said, "Mom, will you come and just hold me and let me cry? I want you to hold me." She said, "I wanted to but I didn't know if you wanted me to."

So we sat there on the floor and hugged and cried. I told her all about the hurt little girl who tried to always smile and not let anyone know how lonely she felt. We cried some more. Then we prayed. We prayed that Jesus would heal the hurt and replace the pain with love. Then I said, "You know, Mom, ever since I was a little girl I've always wanted to go into the kitchen and bake a pie with you." So we went into the kitchen and baked two pies!

I realize now that if I had told Mom that I needed her before, she would have been there for me. If I had shared the struggles and pain, she would have supported me. But I held it in and she never knew how badly I needed her.

I've learned a lot by the experience we shared that day. Not only is our relationship deeper and closer, but I have a new courage to share my real feelings with others.

Though emotional honesty is sometimes difficult and frightening, it is usually better than stuffing our emotions in a gunny sack to pretend we've gotten rid of them. We need to have heart-to-heart talks with the emotionally significant people in our lives. When we're hurt we need to say so. When we're angry we need to get it off our chests—as diplomatically as possible. When we feel affection we need to show it. The compass of the self helps us to stay emotionally connected to God and others. When we get stuck we need to pray for help.

In the case of anger or resentment, Paul said, "Be angry but do not sin; do not let the sun go down on your anger" (Eph 4:26).

The Lesson of the Rose

The rose symbolizes the process of growth, development and flowering into fullness of being. Consider how the wonderful and mysterious action of God's Spirit of creation works with irresistible pressure from within the rose—guiding its transformation from a closed bud to a fully open bloom. The rose meditation can be done in a group. I suggest that a blooming rose be passed from person to person before the meditation, so that each can see, touch and smell the rose.

> To begin the meditation, imagine one stem with leaves and a rosebud. The bud appears green because the sepals are closed, but at the very top a rose-colored point can be seen. Let us visualize this vividly, holding the image in the center of our consciousness.
>
> Now begins a slow movement: the sepals start to separate little by little, turning their points outward and revealing the rose-hued petals, which are still closed. The sepals continue to open until we can see the whole of the tender bud. The petals follow suit and slowly separate, until a perfect fully-opened rose is seen.
>
> At this stage, let us try to smell the perfume of this rose, inhaling its characteristic scent; so delicate, sweet and delicious. Let us smell it with delight. (It may be recalled that religious language has frequently employed perfume as a symbol, e.g., "the odor of sanctity;" and incense is also used in many religious ceremonies.)
>
> Let us now expand our imagery to include the whole rose-bush, and imagine God's life force that arises in the roots to the flower and originates the process of opening.
>
> Finally, let us identify ourselves with the rose itself or, more precisely, let us introject it into ourselves. Symbolically, we are this flower, this rose. The same life that ani-

mates God's universe and creates the miracle of the rose is producing in us a like, even greater miracle—the awakening and development of our spiritual being and that which radiates from it.[23]

> *Pain, injustice, suffering and evil are fertilizer for vital growth.*

Through this exercise we can effectively foster the inner "flowering" of our personality into the rose petals of love, assertion, weakness and strength. Pain, injustice, suffering and evil are fertilizer for vital growth. Balance, grace and beauty unfold as we become fully alive, Christ-like personalities.

An African Christian named Guambi suffered the murder of his family in the massacre of Leopoldville, yet still managed to become one of the most humble and loving men I've ever known. How did he get over the grief of lost loved ones?

Guambi told me that a Christian is like a rose. God can help even the tragic misfortunes of life to act as fertilizer for vigorous growth in those who seek his will. We can't explain why a tragedy occurs, but with God's help we can learn certain things from it. As we learn, we begin to grow. The newly planted rose bush must allow weeks and even months to assimilate the fertilizer which surrounds its base, and so must we be patient with the growth process.

In time a miraculous transformation occurs. The dung of life is broken down into nutrients which become rich nourishment for new life. This fertilizer is gradually transformed into the beautiful, fragrant blossoms of the rose. The piercing thorns serve to remind us of the cost of wholeness and holiness.

We don't need perfect faith to experience personality transformation, only a mustard seed of faith that God is our Father, Jesus is our Savior and the Holy Spirit is our Comforter and Counselor.

Ten

Befriending Your Unconscious

Charles and Mary are a couple I know who've lived out their religious lives in their heads, not their hearts. Not knowing what the unconscious is and how it could enrich their spiritual lives, they have followed a course of religious rigidity that is leaving them, at the age of fifty, without inspiration from their core selves.

They are proud to be among the most punctual members of their parish. They scrupulously follow the letter of the law. They consider themselves to be among the pious elite in their community. When they discuss their relationship with God, they neither mention feeling touched by God, or personally knowing him.

Charles and Mary possess little or no awareness of personal identity, intimacy with the Lord or loving communion with others. Their primary motivation seems to be copying the well-heeled Catholics in their immediate environment. Their religious and ethical life lacks inspiration from the Holy Spirit. "To be spiritual," writes Cardinal Leo Suenens of Belgium, "is to be always ready to expect the unexpected from God, for God is even now creating anew. We are not prisoners of determinism.... To those who welcome the Spirit there is liberty, joy and trust. Who would dare to say, therefore, that the love and imagination of God are exhausted?"[24]

In the process of developing spiritual depth, we find out that God uses our unconscious to help us know him and ourselves more deeply. We learn to sense the unseen presence of the divine in our total being—even in the depths of the unconscious. Failure to accept our unconscious core impulses deprives us of wholeness and leaves us stuck in rigid roles.

What Is the Unconscious, Anyway?

Consciousness is what you're thinking or experiencing at any given moment: the doctor's appointment; the street light changing from red to green; your kid's baseball game. The conscious mind analyzes needs and situations, predicts logical consequences and makes decisions.

Picture a sailboat skimming along the surface of the ocean. The boat is like consciousness—what you're thinking, remembering or planning. Now picture the huge body of water beneath the sailboat. The ocean is like the unfathomable depths of the unconscious.

The longer I counsel, the more I discover the spiritual power of the unconscious. I define the unconscious as the *ultimate data bank of one's personal experiences throughout life; the carrier of a person's inner blueprints for a fulfilling destiny.* The unconscious carries within it the potency for fleshing out one's talents, gifts and destiny in life. We can try to ignore or hide from this depth dimension of personality—but we can never get rid of it.

Our unconscious is more all-encompassing and smarter than our conscious mind. The unconscious draws from countless billions of body and brain cells; our conscious mind draws from a tiny fraction of brain cells in our neo-cortex, where conscious thinking originates. Our conscious mind is good for mental gymnastics, but *the unconscious represents our entire genetic and spiritual capability—mind, heart, body and spirit.*

"There is more to knowing," writes Father McBrien, "than reasoning alone. We are moved not only by external events but also by the dark and utterly mysterious world of the unconscious."[25]

We can befriend our own unconscious, and welcome it to a warm hearth of dialogue with our conscious minds.

The unconscious is like the eighty-eight keys of a piano. As long as all eighty-eight keys are pliable, the conscious mind can play any tune it wishes. But if some of the keys are suppressed—held tightly in place and prevented from moving—then the tunes we can play are proportionately limited. This robs us of the piano's full potential.

When we draw freely from the storehouse of the unconscious, we vastly extend the data base of the conscious mind. But the unconscious takes on a negative character when we disown parts of it and pretend they don't exist. As growing Christians we don't need to try to wipe out the voice of the unconscious. Martin Marty, of the University of Chicago, writes: "Catholicism...is a faith that teaches me that because you have a core or center, you can make room for a variety of apparently competitive and interactive elements."[26] We can befriend our own unconscious, and welcome it to a warm hearth of dialogue with our conscious minds.

David is a biblical example of a man who tried to sweep his unconscious under the carpet. Scripture calls David a man after God's own heart. He demonstrated faith when he fought Goliath, courage when he led troops into battle, and compassion when he played his harp to soothe King Saul's fits of rage and melancholia. But later on, when David became king, his conscious mind became narrowly focused on one pursuit: having sex with Bathsheba and plotting to have her husband killed. David ceased being a man after God's heart.

What happened? When David's conscious mind became obsessed with taking Bathsheba, he totally blocked out the betrayal and treachery involved. But his unconscious knew. After David committed the evil deeds, God sent Nathan the prophet to speak to him. Nathan told a parable about a rich man who stole the only lamb a poor man owned. David did not realize at first that this was a reference to his acts of adultery and murder. David became furious and declared that such a man should be put to death. Suddenly, Nathan exclaimed, *"You are the man!"* In an instant, David's unconscious became fully conscious. He collapsed in shame and remorse (cf. 2 Sam 12:1-15).

Your unconscious is the sum total of all that you have experienced, felt and learned in life— a vast reservoir of wisdom to help your conscious mind be faithful to your total being.

Our unconscious knows whether we do good or evil; it knows whether we've recovered from past traumas or avoided them; and it knows what career we should choose to find God's will. *Our unconscious knows who we really are and what is the next right thing to do.*

A thirty-five-year old woman named Theresa had endured great difficulty in her marital sex life. She seemed shut down to the sensations and positive emotions of sex. At a conscious level, she rationalized that she was responsive, although she never experienced an orgasm in fifteen years of marriage. This baffled her conscious mind, but her unconscious knew exactly what the problem was. One night she dreamed about herself as a teenager being sexually molested by her grandfather. The dream was so real that it shocked her into wakefulness. The unconscious had finally broken into consciousness. Over the next weeks, she recalled dozens of actual events in which her grandfather had sexually molested her.

Now her conscious mind had real information to work with. She sought therapy to tell her story to someone who could understand. She talked to her sister and one cousin who had also been molested by her grandfather. Finally she confronted him directly. After facing and feeling all of these repressed memories—and acting on them in a positive manner—this woman's sexuality blossomed in her marriage. Her body, heart and spirit were reunited with her conscious mind, after years of being shut down.

Your unconscious is the sum total of all that you have experienced, felt and learned in life—a vast reservoir of wisdom to help your conscious mind be faithful to your total being. While some people suppress (sit on) or repress (bury) the voice of their unconscious, it is always wiser to hear what it has to say. The Creator designed the conscious and unconscious to work in rhythmic dialogue. The term "centering prayer" was inspired by the Trappist monk Thomas Merton, who stressed in his earlier writings that the only way to come into contact with the living God is to go to one's center and from that point to get in touch with God. It is a spirituality of interiority, of going deeply into oneself in order to tap the divine reality present within.

A woman named Theresa was nominated as president of her women's auxiliary group. While her conscious mind focused on the prestige of the office, her unconscious brought to her body sensations of tension and anxiety. The voice of her unconscious was saying, "You're already stressed out with other obligations." After she declined the nomination, she felt a wave of peace flow through her.

Joseph Goldbrunner's essay on "Holiness and Wholeness" suggests that the incarnation teaches there is a wholeness to human life, which encompasses the body as well as the spirit. Each person must get in touch with the universe of the unconscious. To live a spiritually healthy life, one must live one's own inner truth in response to the Holy Spirit. "One must consciously come to terms with the irrational forces within oneself, incorporating them into the total life of the soul."[27]

In American culture, society's "shoulds" imprinted on the conscious mind sometimes drown out the wisdom of our unconscious. They tell us that we should succeed no matter what; we should be strong and not weak; we should please those around us; and we should obey authority even if it harms us. If we overrule our inner truth in Christ, the unconscious will sound a warning by giving us ulcers, headaches, high blood pressure, nightmares, panic attacks and depression. Lacking the eloquence of conscious thought, the unconscious uses the primitive language of sensation, emotion and bodily symptoms. As soon as we hear the message of the unconscious, and make appropriate new decisions, these problems usually vanish.

Christians in tune with their unconscious and the voice of the Holy Spirit live one day at a time, and value the creative dialogue between conscious thoughts and unconscious intuition.

Here are four ways to tap into the wisdom of your unconscious and benefit from what it's trying to tell you:

- build a dialogue with your boredom
- face your inner conflicts
- give your bodily ailment a voice and learn what it has to say
- change your nightmares into dreams come true

Building a Dialogue with Boredom

As a child, I was fascinated with people and personalities. I wanted to know what made people tick and to discover more about myself. This intrigue with the psyche came from my unconscious and provided a major clue to the career that would excite me as an adult. But I turned a deaf ear. My parents wanted me to become a physician. Anything else was unacceptable. In high school and college I focused my conscious mind on obeying them.

What happened? In my senior year of college I developed a severe depression. The Holy Spirit in my unconscious, knowing about my true heart's desires, was revealing to me that I was in the wrong field. My symptom of depression was warning me that I was not paying attention to God's will for me.

I graduated with a Bachelor of Science degree and entered medical school. The voice of my unconscious grew louder, as though to warn me I was on the wrong track. Over the next several months I felt terribly bored about memorizing the facts of the body. I yearned to understand what makes people tick. Finally, I respected my boredom enough to leave my scholarship and switch my career to counseling and psychotherapy.

A great peace welled up in me the day I decided to become a healer of the soul instead of the body. For the past twenty-five years, I have been blessed to realize the deeper desires of my heart.

The unconscious mediates rather than hinders God's guidance. Biblical characters were often inspired by dreams and visions precisely because their conscious minds would have rejected God's plan. For those who trust him, God uses what lies hidden in the depths of their unconscious as a resource for guiding the conscious mind toward doing his will.

Thomas Merton writes: "Why do we have to spend our lives being something we would never want to be? Why do we waste our time doing things which, if we only stopped to think about them, are just the opposite of what we were made for? We cannot be ourselves unless we know ourselves. But self-knowledge is impossible when thoughtless and automatic activity keeps our souls in confusion. We cannot begin to know ourselves until we can see the real reasons why we do the things we do."[28]

Facing Inner Conflicts

Several months ago I was in a session with a rather passive and dependent woman. She seemed especially vague about what might be contributing to her tension headaches and to a painful sense of self-consciousness around her own home.

I couldn't seem to grasp the crux of the matter, using only normal probing techniques—probably because she herself had so little awareness of what was tormenting her.

So I said, "If we picture you sitting on your favorite sofa, and relaxing for just a moment and if we say that your deepest problem has a color—which color would it be?"

"Black," she said.

"Okay," I said. "Now what kind of shape is it?"

"It's a big black blob. It fills most of the room, and I feel smothered by it."

"And how does it feel if you touch it?" I asked.

"I never touch it.... I'm too afraid," she said.

I noticed that her knuckles were white from being closed so tightly into fists. "What do your hands want to do with the blob?" I inquired.

"They want to get it out of here! I'm sick to death of being smothered by it!"

"If we gave the big smothering black blob a name, what would it be?" I asked.

There was a very long pause, the kind of pause which shows that the unconscious mind is on a bio-computer search scanning all possible responses, before making a final choice.

"It seems to be...my mother!"

At this moment she opened her eyes and looked at me in a surprised manner. "Is that what this is all about?" she stammered. "Is this depression all about my mother?"

"That's what your unconscious has just told us," I replied. "I believe your unconscious has known that your mother has been smothering you for a long time. You just didn't know how to listen to it."

As we explored the hypothesis, she said, "My mother is impossible to please. She knows exactly where my furniture should be placed, and how to raise my kids—even how my meals should be cooked and how my husband should be treated. I can't ever do anything right!"

"How long do you want to keep the big, smothering black blob in your life?" I asked.

"I want to change it right now!" she exclaimed.

"Close your eyes and relax," I coached. "You've made a decision to change things, to get out from under the blob. Now be creative. Can you see the blob?"

"Yes," she said.

"You're free to do anything you wish in your mind's eye. What are you doing?"

A smile lit up her face. "I'm getting a broom from the closet, and sweeping like crazy."

"How is it going?"

"I need something stronger," she said. "Now I'm using the vacuum cleaner, and I'm getting more of it. This feels good!"

"What is the blob doing?" I asked.

She frowned triumphantly. "It doesn't want to leave, but I am going to make it go. There, I've got most of it out now," she announced after another minute.

"Can you come up with something stronger to get rid of the last traces?" I asked.

"No," she said, as she opened her eyes and looked at me. "I don't want to get any more out. I feel great with all the new space. I don't want the blob to go completely away."

"You've shown a tremendous amount of courage today. You came face to face with your mom and you took a strong stand for autonomy. I am curious how you will apply this new knowledge and power for improving your life. But I also hear you saying that you do still want some kind of relationship with your mother—just not a lop-sided one."

"That's right," she chimed in. "I'm not letting her push me around anymore. I'm going to tell her to keep her criticisms to herself. And if she can back off and treat me more like an adult, then we can still be friends."

"And if she can't?" I couldn't help but ask.

"Then she'll have to be alone until she does," she stated. *"I'm not afraid of the black blob anymore."*

Giving Our Bodily Ailment a Voice

Michelle was a high school teacher in her mid-thirties who came to see me about chronic weight problems. I used a technique that gave her bodily ailment—in this case the extra pounds—a voice. Shortly, Michelle heard what her unconscious had been trying to say for fifteen years. Here's Michelle's story in her own words:

> In my late twenties, after my second child was born, I began gaining weight for the first time in my life. This is an awareness I have now, but was then in total denial about. I'd look at pictures of myself and think that's not really what I look like—the camera must have been at the wrong angle. By my mid-thirties, I was overweight by thirty pounds. I began to suffer from nausea and abdominal pain. At thirty-five I underwent gall bladder surgery, but that didn't solve my weight problem. I entered therapy with Dr. Montgomery to get ideas about losing weight. In our second session, he put a chair across from me and said it represented my extra weight. He told me to talk to the weight and then reverse roles with the weight by sitting in the other chair and talking back to myself. By moving back and forth between my conscious self and my weight, the following dialogue occurred:
>
> ME: I don't like you, but I can't get rid of you. You make me feel ugly and depressed.
>
> MY WEIGHT: Don't blame me. I'm not your scapegoat. I just want you to face your real feelings.

Befriending Your Unconscious / 129

ME: I need to blame something for my unhappiness. It's all your fault. If only you'd get lost, I'd be happy.

MY WEIGHT: Listen to yourself. You're always whining. You need me here so you don't have to face what's really bothering you.

ME: You're what's bothering me.

MY WEIGHT: No I'm not. Your husband is. You feel angry at him. You know he doesn't listen to you or even show you love.

ME: That's true. I do feel depressed about our marriage.

MY WEIGHT: Then do something about it. Quit eating your feelings and start expressing them!

I felt stunned when these last words came out of me. Dr. Montgomery stopped the dialogue and asked me what I'd just learned from my unconscious. I stammered that I could see the connection between my floundering marriage and my compulsive eating.

Over several months of therapy, I gradually integrated my unconscious with my conscious life. When I felt put down or ignored by my husband, I expressed my feelings instead of heading to the refrigerator. When I felt the need for closeness, I approached Steve instead of avoiding him. I prayed and worked on improving our marriage instead of numbing myself through overeating. As we developed a more fair and loving relationship, my depression lifted and my out-of-control eating diminished.

As the pounds melted away, my body and emotions became friends, not enemies. I began to see my unconscious as a treasure house of wisdom that I can draw from every day. When we finished therapy, Dr. Montgomery recommended Overeaters Anonymous as a good support group so I could keep learning how to make my unconscious conscious.

The technique of placing your symptom in a chair and shuttling back and forth to learn what it can teach you, can be used with sleep disturbances, sexual problems, eating disorders, circulatory stresses, skin rashes and addictions. We may be surprised by the unconscious meaning of such maladies, but tapping the wisdom of the unconscious boosts the process of recovery.

Changing Our Nightmares into Dreams Come True

"I have a nightmare that keeps coming back no matter what I do," said Tony as he jumped up from my leather office chair and began pacing. "Thirty years have passed. Why won't it go away, Dr. Dan? I still hear the mortars exploding and weapons firing all around me. It's terrifying. And the pigs. I can't get rid of the pigs!"

"What emotion is coming through you right now?" I asked.

"Fear. I'm shaking. That's why I can't sit down. I did a really bad thing in that Vietcong village. After the mortar attack, I went berserk and killed all their pigs—about fifty of them.

"The attack wasn't their fault, but I got furious and wanted to strike out at something. So I blew away their pigs."

"Is this the first time you've talked about it?" I asked.

"No, a long time ago I told a priest in confession, but the nightmares didn't change. I wake up screaming and sweating. My wife tries to help me but she can't. I've tried sleeping pills and just staying awake. Nothing helps!"

"That's because you're not listening to the message of the dream. You can't control your unconscious with will power or medication. You need to hear what it's trying to tell you. What are you feeling now?" I asked.

"Shame," Tony said and sat down. His head sunk low, almost between his knees. "I was so mad about the shelling. You feel so helpless when you can't see the enemy and shrapnel is flying everywhere. My best buddy got killed that day. I felt so much rage I slaughtered all the pigs. Then I felt so ashamed. How can I make this nightmare go away?"

"That's what we're here for," I said. "Let's face your unconscious and give those buried feelings and memories a fresh hearing. Those pigs have been trying to tell you something for thirty years."

His face flushed and furrows of tension appeared on his forehead. "I'm afraid to think about it. What if I go crazy?"

"You do go crazy in your nightmares. But if we think about it here, you'll be safe."

I asked Tony to relax in the chair, take a few deep breaths and to picture the pigs in his mind's eye. "What do the pigs want to tell you?" I asked.

"They're saying, 'Why'd you kill us? We didn't harm you. Why'd you make the villagers go starving?'"

"What do you want to say back?"

"I want to say, 'I didn't want to be in that war. Death was everywhere. I was just a kid. I went crazy that day. I killed you pigs in a rage. I'm sorry—I feel so guilty.'" Tony began to weep softly.

"Tony," I said, "you're doing the right thing by facing these painful feelings. They can't hurt you now. The war's been over a long time. Life in that village is back to normal. But your unconscious is coaxing you to do something new—something creative—to balance out the evil of the war. That's why this dream keeps coming back; it's like a stuck record needing to be pushed forward so the rest of the tune can be played.

"What can I do?" he asked.

"Use your imagination to go back to that village with a positive mission in mind. Turn your M-16 into a symbol of peace. Turn your helmet into a normal hat. Bring about some beneficial changes. What do you want to do?"

"The people are very poor. There's no school in the village."

"Can you build one?"

"Yes. I'm using my walkie-talkie to call for bulldozers and cement mixers."

"Good. What else?"

"The people need medicine and a place for treatment."

"What do you want to do?"

"I'm building a hospital now. And making sure it has plenty of supplies."

"Good. Feel your compassion flow through your whole body. You are blessing them, not harming them. Is there anything else you want to do before you leave the village?"

"Yes, I want to apologize for the pigs I killed a long time ago," he said, tension coming back into his face.

"Go ahead."

"I'm sorry for killing your pigs. I didn't want to hurt anybody. I know it was wrong. Please forgive me." A couple of tears streamed down his cheeks.

"What's happening?" I asked.

"They're saying that it's okay, that everybody suffered in the war. They're saying they don't hold it against me. A couple of people are shaking my hand."

"And the pigs?"

"They're back alive. They look happy. I'm building them a fence."

"Okay," I said, "It's time to leave the village and come back here. Open your eyes." Tony blinked a few times and heaved a big sigh.

"You mean that's going to help me get over these nightmares?" he asked, skepticism showing in his voice.

"Yes," I said. "Tonight I want you to replay this new version of your visit to the village before you go to sleep. The Holy Spirit in your unconscious is redeeming your horrible experience—showing you how to care for the villagers instead of killing their pigs."

The nightmare recurred four more times, each time with less force. Tony kept turning negative memories into positive actions. We would pray during sessions for the healing of his memories. After the fourth week of counseling, Tony announced that in his latest dream he entered the village as a friend bearing gifts for the people and their children. They accepted him with great joy. The practical spin-off was that Tony became more relaxed and nurturing around his friends and family.

Cardinal Suenens writes: "In psychological terms, we could say that it is the voice of the subconscious rising to God, finding a manner of praying which is analogous to other expressions of our subconscious in dreams, laughter, tears, painting or dance. This prayer within the depths of our being heals at a profound yet often perceptible level hidden psychological wounds that impede the full development of our interior life."[29]

The lesson of this chapter is to identity with that which haunts us, not in order to fight it off, but to take it into ourselves. It represents some rejected element in our being. Denied parts of us take on a tormenting character until we invite them into the warm hearth of dialogue to hear what they have to say. As soon as we assimilate what was formerly split off, peace floods our soul. We are made wiser for accepting more of our real selves, and for surrendering more of our total being to God.

Eleven

Images of God

WE ALL PROJECT ONTO GOD AN image derived from our early experiences with our own parents. It's no surprise. Our parents are our first experience with God-like entities. If they relate to us with a balance of affection (love), firmness (assertion), empathy (weakness), and consistency (strength), it's likely we'll develop a positive image of God and a loving trust in him.

On the other hand, our parents may embody imbalanced and exaggerated personality patterns, such as those described in this book. Then we are prone to distort and distrust our image of God. Think for a moment how your early experiences of your dad or mom are unconsciously influencing your assumptions about God to this day.

Leah told me that she trusted God with all her heart. Yet this young college woman always seemed apprehensive when she spoke of God. Her eyes would dart back and forth and her voice would get tinny. Her hands would curve in slightly and tense up. I became convinced that her feelings of closeness to God seemed well-intentioned, but untrue. As one of Shakespeare's characters said, "Methinks the lady protests too much."

After some probing I found out that Leah was raised in a strict religious home. Her mother often slapped her young daughter for saying or doing the "wrong" thing. The mother constantly admonished Leah that if she wasn't God's perfect little angel, he would throw her out of heaven. Knowing that she wasn't perfect, little Leah unconsciously assumed that God was always upset and displeased with her—that he was a stern and angry judge, just like her mother.

When I first suggested to Leah that she was unconsciously living out of the same fearful orientation she had learned as a child, she flatly denied it. When I said that she might be forcing herself to love God out of a deep-seated fear of punishment, she thought this was incredible. "How could such a thing be?" she said. "I go to Mass every Sunday and pray diligently throughout each day."

I respected Leah's doubts about my interpretation, but her body revealed that she had shut down to a significant degree. Her hands were cool to the touch. She seldom looked to the right or left. She never smiled. She constantly fidgeted with her hands during conversations. Her voice betrayed no emotional inflection. Leah was a person who had not allowed her unconscious to become conscious, so that she could clarify her vision of God.

When I described her mother's methods of discipline as mean, excessive and heartless, this young woman would glance around the room as though expecting to see her mother's scowling face. She'd look scared to death, but then would dutifully seek to justify the abuse as having been for Leah's own good. "Mom just wanted to protect me from evil things. She hit me to make me behave."

How could I convince Leah of the inner truth that her body revealed—that she had lived in shame and terror as a child, and that these long-buried feelings were still very active? How could I help her move along the journey of wholeness if she remained deaf to her unconscious as communicated by her body?

What I had in my favor was that Leah *wanted to be healed.* She was sick of being frightened of classmates, professors and everyone else. She was tired of hiding in her room whenever she wasn't holing up in the library. She was at the end of her rope with anxiety from avoiding sports events, social occasions and dating. She had secretly prayed for years for God to make her into a normal human being. Now was her chance. Though it was hard for her to hear it, Leah took what I was saying to heart.

During one session I asked her to try an experiment. I asked Leah to say a prayer to God in front of me. I asked her to pray for God to guide and bless us in the course of her therapy. Leah agreed. As soon as she bowed her head, her lips pursed, her shoulders hunched up and her knuckles began to turn white from the pressure between her tightly interlocked fingers. Her body was riddled with tension as she spoke. She began formulating a prayer which was sincere but very formal, yet her words revealed how she *longed* to feel close to God and trust him.

I interrupted Leah in the middle of her prayer and asked her to look at the whites of her knuckles. Her eyes widened with surprise. I asked her to listen to the formality and tension in her voice. Leah's mouth dropped open. All at once her face radiated understanding. "I *am* uptight, aren't I? This is how I *always* feel when I pray!"

"Is this how you felt when you were around your mother as a child?" I asked.

"Yes," Leah admitted. "This is exactly how I felt—like I was going to get swatted any minute and I never knew why."

"Do you see now how your image of God is the spitting image of your mother? You live in constant fear that he'll swat you if you're not his perfect little angel."

"Oh my word, it's true!" she exclaimed. Leah stared straight ahead for a few moments and then looked back at me. "Can I get over this?"

"Of course you can," I told her. *"Awareness* is the first step in personality growth. Now that you're aware that your unconscious has stored feelings of shame and fear since childhood, we can start to get rid of them. You can discover that God actually loves you dearly."

As Leah took a deep breath, her whole body seemed to relax. Then a real smile slowly spread across her face. "I never thought God would answer my prayers *this* way, but let's go for it, Dr. Dan."

During her year of therapy, Leah learned how to use diplomacy and firmness in standing up to her mother, how to express the full range of her emotions, to speak up in the classroom, to enjoy sports and social events, to date and relate with men, and to surrender to the non-intrusive, all-encompassing, *healthy love of God*. She became so outgoing that she even got a CB short-wave radio for her car and used as her handle "Huggy Bear." Having courageously taken the risks for growth, Leah was experiencing the payoff of a balanced personality coupled with an intimate image of God.

As college valedictorian, Leah gave the keynote address to the faculty and her graduating class. After the ceremony I saw her wading through the crowd with tears streaming down her face. She grabbed me with both arms and said, "I love you, Dr. Dan. I wouldn't be here without you and God."

I responded, "Leah, you're the best daughter a parent could ever have. I believe in you and so does Jesus." This mature young woman burst into a smile and that was the last time I ever saw her.

Father Albert Haase writes: "Our image of God is one of the most, if not the most, important aspects of the spiritual life. Our God-image shapes and colors everything about our personal spirituality: from why we pray to how we understand suffering and evil in the world. Unhealthy images of God elicit unhealthy behavior. Indeed, a particular image of God can be the very reason someone leaps to holiness or walks at a mere snail's pace in the spiritual life."[30]

Negative projections from our unconscious will influence our spiritual life until the day we face ourselves more authentically and come to perceive God in more healthy ways.

Some clergy believe that indoctrination gives people the correct view of God. But indoctrination doesn't even phase the unconscious processes at work in the personality. Indoctrination is like branding a cow with a branding iron—it leaves a mark on the hide, but doesn't touch the cow's interior. We must open the height and depth of our personality to Christ—conscious and unconscious—so that we are drawn to him and lovingly choose his Lordship. Our hearts, minds and bodies need the Holy Spirit's renewal throughout life.

Knowing this, St. Paul wrote: "For I am sure that neither death, nor life, nor angels, nor principalities, nor things present, nor things to come, nor powers, nor height, nor depth, nor anything else in all creation, will be able to separate us from the love of God in Christ Jesus our Lord" (Rom 8:38-39). The pathway to wholeness, then, is through risking self-awareness and self-expression. We need courage to form a living friendship and ongoing dialogue with the Lord.

The following section discusses how each of the four personality perspectives described in this book distort the image of God. Prayerfully find which exaggerated views of God have unconsciously influenced your God-image. Ask the Holy Spirit to help you trade them for a more accurate perception of God that includes his intelligence, love, compassion, graciousness, fidelity and strength.[31]

The Dependent Distortion of God

Leah exemplified an individual stuck with a dependent view of God—her God-image portrayed a stern and unforgiving authority figure. In the dependent perspective, God is all-knowing, all-seeing and basically mean. "He knows if you've been naughty or nice, so be good for goodness sake." We obey him out of an unconscious fear of being punished. On the outside we smile and talk positively about God. But on the inside we are extremely insecure about his love for us. We try hard to please him, yet secretly feel guilty and depressed that we're never enough.

An Episcopal priest came to see me for counseling. He had served in the ministry for a decade and felt burned out.

"I don't know why I'm so depressed," he said. "I have a loving wife, a good teenage boy and my ministry is successful. I get along with everybody. People like me and treat me well. But I'm terribly depressed underneath it all."

"Let me ask you this," I said. "What is your image of God?"

"He is a magnificent and all-powerful being. I should serve him at all times. I should love everyone in my parish. I should never make a mistake."

"Do you have trouble saying no to people?"

"I never say no. God wouldn't want me to say no," he said.

"Do you take on more responsibilities than you can handle, so that nobody will be disappointed?"

"Yes, all the time. I'm supposed to be a loving servant."

"Do you need constant assurance that you are doing okay, that you are a good person?"

"Yes, I suppose so. I certainly don't want to offend anyone."

"One last question. Are you on your best behavior right now so I'll think you're a nice guy?"

He squirmed a bit in the black leather chair. "How did you know that?" he asked.

"Because your picture of God leaves out the great reality that he loves *you!* I believe if you develop a more balanced perception of God, you'll feel freer to express yourself with people and not live under the gun. You'll become more like Christ himself, who said that he didn't seek people's approval or disapproval."

It took this priest several months to review his image of God and seek to balance it. In doing so, he became aware that he had unconsciously modeled his image of God on his own father, who was rather aloof and demanding. In private devotions, he asked the Holy Spirit to show him the loving side of God. He told me later that his inner spiritual self now felt sprung loose, helping him find new strength for his ministry and joy in God's love for him.

The Aggressive Distortion of God

Aggressive people are convinced that God is wrathful, militant and out to punish all who do not adopt their particular brand of Christianity. They expound on God's judgment, not his mercy and grace. They carry out grand inquisitions against those who express dissimilar views. They wage war against secular culture and downgrade other traditions within the larger Body of Christ. They even persecute clergy or religious within their own ranks. In the unbalanced view of the aggressive perspective, God is a God of vengeance.

King Saul had these tendencies. He made people around him walk on eggshells. He set himself up as god junior. The need for absolute power consumed him. He would explode with wrath at a moment's notice. Like Saul, dictatorial and domineering Christians harm those around them. Underneath their facades of bravado, these individuals secretly harbor inferiority complexes. Some suffer severe neurosis.

The Church of Vatican II strongly challenges the aggressive God-image. Vatican II affirms the Catholic Church as a "pluralistic Church open to pluralism, a modern Church open to modernity, an ecumenical Church open to the whole wide world, a living Church open to new life and to the change it brings, and requires a catholic Church open in principle to all truth and to every value."[32] The wrath, intolerance, suspicion, divisiveness and strife of the aggressive image of God is out. The God who creates and sustains us, draws near to our heart's desires, and empowers us to do his will is in.

The Withdrawn Distortion of God

In the withdrawn perspective, we are nervous about intimate encounters with the Holy Trinity. We avoid emotional closeness with anyone. Jonah was such an individual. He ran away from God's inner voice. It took time alone in a whale's belly for him to reconsider. What God was seeking to communicate to Jonah was his tender love for the people of Ninevah. Withdrawn people suffer from the Jonah complex: they run away from their own great calling.

"God wants me to live a lonely life as penance for my sins." "I feel guilty whenever I think about God, so I try to stay as far from him as possible."

A story is told of a man in a flood who found himself stranded on a church steeple. He prayed vigorously for God to rescue him. A boat came by and the captain yelled at him to jump in, but the man was too afraid. A raft floated by. He could have jumped on, but it seemed a bit too far. Finally, a helicopter hovered overhead and dropped down a ladder, but he was afraid to fly and rejected the opportunity.

The church then collapsed and the man drowned. He awakened in heaven and immediately whined that he had prayed to be rescued, but to no avail.

Suddenly the voice of God said, "Who do you think sent the boat, the raft, and the helicopter?"

Withdrawn individuals need to outgrow their image of God as disinterested, distant and rejecting. They need to discover that he is kind, accepting and truly loving. Indeed, God's special hobby is blessing the meek of the earth.

The Controlling Distortion of God

People with the controlling perspective believe that God demands conformity, criticizing anything innovative or original. Self-control becomes the paramount issue in religious life. Religious rules must be followed to the letter of the law. But the authority of Christ is not that of a controlling, authoritarian personality, but of a supreme lover of the human soul. His authority attracts people to the grace of God.

Since the joyful promptings of the Holy Spirit are lost to them, controllers accomplish admirable goals in unconsciously self-serving ways. Because of their grim and overly strict approach to God, they are emotionally insensitive to those around them. They miss or ignore vital aspects of the spiritual life: love, play and fellowship.

Father van Kaam writes: "I continually drive myself to increasing religious perfection and regularity, to more and more magnificent manifestations of apostolic fervor, in order to display my superiority in saintliness. The source of my efforts is not my love of God, but overwhelming anxiety and the secret feeling of worthlessness at the root of my existence. Nevertheless, I may believe that my remarkable regularity is the fruit of holiness."[33]

Christ doesn't need superior know-it-alls to feed his sheep.

Christ doesn't need superior know-it-alls to feed his sheep. No one is called to be a paragon of virtue to the flock. Controllers need to open themselves to experience God's grace, fun and humor. God accepts real weaknesses far more than controllers realize. He loves and appreciates the uniqueness of persons. If we surrender to him, he accepts us beyond our achievements or failures. He shows us how to become balanced personalities, not through striving for perfection, but by letting go and letting God.

Living out the principle of spiritual love that is central to Jesus' own personality requires being our real selves and cultivating patience as others do the same. The living God desires creative fidelity to our unique calling, openness to develop the dynamics of a healthy personality and courage to follow where ever he may lead us.

Not only is God healthy and self-sustaining, but he is interpersonally motivated for friendship and fellowship. In Jesus, the Father manifests an outgoing spirit of altruistic love, called *agape* in the New Testament. The Lord isn't interested in an elitist band of in-crowders, but is ecumenically minded, always seeking the lost, the lonely and the excluded. I dare say that God is far more loving of humanity than we Christians are capable of becoming, but we can give it a try!

The people of God grow best in an atmosphere which fosters intimacy, identity and loving community. They grow by the power of the Holy Spirit.

Twelve

The Prayer Compass

SATURDAY AFTERNOON DR. O'CONNELL stood on our front porch speaking to Mom. She nodded her head. Was I in for trouble?

At twelve years old, I eyed Dr. O'Connell warily through the front window. Was it the frisbee I threw the day before that glanced off his windshield? Would Dad belt my bottom when he got home?

I scooted upstairs to hide in my bedroom as Mom came into the living room. "Danny, come here!" My heart pounded as I crept back down the stairs.

"Danny, Dr. O'Connell just offered you a wonderful job in August. He wants you to water his roses for three weeks while he's in Europe. But you'll have to be careful. It's the hottest month of the year."

Of course, I wanted to play, not work. "I have to play Little League," I wailed. "We practice every day!"

"It'll just take an hour and he'll pay you seventy-five cents a day. You're the oldest boy on the block, so he's got to count on you. You should be proud. Dr. O'Connell's rose garden is famous throughout New Mexico."

Seventy-five cents a day. A *movie and a bag of buttered popcorn,* I thought.

"Okay," I said. "How do you water roses?"

"Go to his house tomorrow at noon. He'll show you. You're a lucky dog. He's got a hundred beautiful roses from all over the world!"

At noon I traipsed down the long block to Dr. O'Connell's Victorian home. The house loomed three stories high. Four pine trees towered above the front yard. I wondered what the back looked like.

Dr. O'Connell met me at the door and smiled. We walked around to a huge white gate. "Here's the key under this brick, Danny," he said. "I keep it locked so that nobody can harm the roses."

"Yes sir," I said.

We walked through the gate into another world. Red, orange, white, maroon, pink, yellow. Wow! A maze of trails meandered among the graded tiers of railroad ties. *A jungle of roses,* I thought. The sweetness struck my nostrils. I followed Dr. O'Connell from one circular steppingstone to another as we made our way among the roses. Each rose had a deep hole around its base for water storage. "That's the Eiffel Tower rose," he said, pointing. "Over there is a Tropicana.... Here is Mr. Lincoln."

He looked back at me. "Danny, you must water each rose until the trough is full. The sun is scorching hot this time of year."

I fidgeted. I wanted to leave as soon as possible so that I could break in my brand new baseball glove.

The trail around the garden and back to the gate seemed a mile long. "I'll give you seventy-five cents a day," he said. "Let's round it off to sixteen dollars for three weeks."

"Okay," I said. The money had grabbed my attention in the first place. I could almost feel the sixteen crunchy dollar bills in my pocket. I'd be rich.

Dr. O'Connell stooped over, squinted, and looked deep in my eyes. "Danny, don't miss a single day."

"Yes sir," I said. We shook hands. I trotted off to oil my new baseball mitt and work in the pocket with my fist.

Dr. O'Connell left for Europe that Monday.

I watered the plants every day that first week. Reading the labels attached to each stem kept my attention through the hour-and-a-half ordeal. Blaze. Double Delight. Sutter's Gold. The Fairy. Queen Elizabeth. I'd swat flies and watch the bumblebees and butterflies.

The second week boredom set in. On Monday I skimped on each flower, finishing them all in thirty minutes. All I could think about was the game against the Kiwanis Cardinals that afternoon. I'd be the starting pitcher.

Two days later we played the Rotary Mad Dogs. On Friday it dawned on me that I had missed several waterings. The rose jungle had become a huge burden. How thirsty could they be anyhow? They all looked fine when I watered them on Monday. When an occasional guilt feeling rippled through my belly, I reasoned, *"Later... I'll go over there later."*

On Monday of the third week I noticed that the flowers looked weak. Petals floated on the water as I hosed each trough. I gave an extra amount of water to help them out.

The rest of the week passed quickly. I sweated under the heat as I pitched a one-hitter against the Hilton Hornets. Two days later I played second base against the Ready Kilowatts. The girl from Seventh street, Marsha, yelled from the stands, "Get a hit, Danny!" I hit a triple, but got thrown out stealing home. Over the weekend I forgot the roses entirely.

Monday morning my heart stopped. I remembered Dr. O'Connell and the rose jungle. *He's coming home today!* I thought. One, two, three, four, five,—six days without water. Will they be okay? A tidal wave of shame smacked me with great force. I was afraid to go look at the garden.

I rode my bike around town all morning trying to take my mind off an impending doom. In practice that afternoon I hit two batters with wild pitches. I ached with anxiety as I rode my bicycle home.

When I arrived, Mom was standing on the porch ringing her hands. She looked awful. I parked my bike and walked up the steps. "Dr. O'Connell came home today," she said. "Danny...all of his roses are dead!"

I felt like vomiting. I wanted to disappear and never be heard from again. I waited for Mom to pronounce a horrible punishment. No allowance for six months. No movies the rest of the year. No playing with friends. She only shook her head and said, "Danny, Dr. O'Connell was crying. I think you broke his heart."

I lay in a fetal position, my heart bursting with remorse. Before going to sleep, I prayed to God that I might make amends to Dr. O'Connell.

No punishment could have been worse than those words. That night a hideous, ugly feeling squirmed in the pit of my stomach. I lay in a fetal position, my heart bursting with remorse. Before going to sleep, I prayed to God that I might make amends to Dr. O'Connell. "Dear Lord, I made a big mistake. I'm very sorry. Please help me to make Dr. O'Connell happy again. In Jesus' name."

But the situation seemed hopeless. I avoided Dr. O'Connell for the next twenty years. Oh, I thought about him—when I saw him walking home from the college or driving in his car. But I made sure that he never saw me. Even as an adult, I hated being reminded of what I had done.

In the meantime, I was developing a more balanced personality. By twenty-nine I had become a doctor of psychology. By thirty-three I had published two books integrating Christianity and psychology. The first book was *Healing Love: How God Works Within the Personality*. God had guided my life so faithfully that one of my major passions was to convince others of his love and good will.

Not many people in my home town knew about the books. I came home from California one Christmas to visit my family. The next morning I went out for breakfast and a voice from the past greeted me at my table. It was Mary O'Connell. I hadn't seen anyone from the O'Connell family in years. "May I join you?" she said.

She sat down and we chatted. Then her face turned more serious. "Danny, did you know that Daddy died last month?"

"I'm sorry, Mary," I said, but inside I felt the old guilt again. I had never made amends for the roses. "I'm very sorry."

"Don't be, Danny. He died knowing God, thanks to you."

I was dumbfounded. "What do you mean?"

"Daddy was an atheist until a few days before he passed away. When I joined the Church and received Christ, Daddy made fun of me. Then Mom and my four sisters were baptized, too, but Daddy wouldn't even come. We all prayed for him for five years, but Daddy kept resisting," Mary continued. "Then one day a friend of his—another professor—gave him a book that caught his attention." She paused, while my curiosity peaked. "Danny, it was *your* book, *Healing Love*."

My heart began to pound as I suddenly recalled my childhood prayer of supplication that somehow, someday, God might use me to bless Dr. O'Connell. "How did he respond to the book?" I asked.

"He read it during the last three days of his life," Mary said. "And he changed, Danny. He began talking to us about Christ. His last day on earth he led us in our first family prayer over dinner. The next morning we found him sitting in his favorite rocker in the study. He looked very peaceful. *Healing Love* was resting on his lap."

Tears flooded my vision. The Holy Spirit seemed to wrap loving arms around Mary and me at the table. Mary was crying, too. Then she smiled. Her big brown eyes sparkled. She said, "Do you know what he wrote in his journal that night?"

"What?"

She spoke gently. "His last entry said, 'I understand now that Christ loves me and gave himself for me. Tonight I have received him. I've never known such peace. *God's healing love is real.'"*

At that moment twenty years of guilt and shame were swept away. I had been unable to do it on my own, but with God's help, in a way I still find incredible, I had at last made amends with Dr. O'Connell.

Father McBrien writes: "Prayer is a conscious, deliberate coming to terms with our actual situation before God."[34] Prayer is always an act of faith and of hope, which is fulfilled in our surrender to the love of God and our honest conversations with him. In a very real sense, personal prayer is talking to God as one would talk to a best friend and confidant.

We may long to form a close relationship with God, but may experience internal barriers stemming from fear or self-consciousness. Here are some questions that may help us understand how to express more of our real selves in prayer to God.

- Can you talk to God without being formal and religious? Do you share spontaneously throughout the day, or do you censor what you believe God would find unacceptable?
- Can you talk to God about every topic without feeling self-conscious, or do you clam up on taboo topics even though you need help and guidance?
- Can you come out with whatever is on your heart without striving to appear nice, proper, moral and good? Or do you need to impress God with your purity, strength, propriety and character?
- Can you talk to God day and night wherever you are? Or do you feel that a church or holy place is the only place where you can commune with God?
- Can you express the broad gamut of your real feelings?

> Or do you feel that God can't handle your anger, depression, anxiety, disillusionment, lust, greed, envy, jealousy, hatred, confusion, frustration, loneliness, fear, sadness or suffering?

If God dares to be your friend, do you dare to be his? If we are not *real* with him, we cannot expect to grow close to him. We must allow God to love us and to accept us exactly as we are. That's how an intimate prayer life begins, and the compass of prayer reminds us how to express our whole selves in a balanced way.

My first divine conversation came at the age of twelve when my agony over the rose jungle caused me to spontaneously cry out for forgiveness and help. A prayer of contrition and supplication welled up from my profound sense of weakness. I cried out to God for help just as the Psalmist did when he wrote: "I cry with my voice to the Lord, with my voice I make supplication to the Lord, I pour out my complaint before him, I tell my trouble before him" (Ps 142:1-2).

As a psychologist, I find that the compass of the self can help people develop a well-rounded prayer life. By praying spontaneously and honestly from the four quadrants of the self, we can come to know rhythm and balance in our prayer life with God, and not get stuck in a rigid pattern.

The Prayer Compass diagram shows how to focus on prayers which arise from love, assertion, weakness or strength, as the situation requires.

Praying From Weakness

Let's start around the compass of prayer with the weakness pole. I first learned how to pray from weakness in my childhood need concerning Dr. O'Connell. On the weakness polarity, we pray for contrition, confession, supplication and surrender.

Through weakness we approach God in need and find that he is "a very present help in trouble" (Ps 46:1). Yet many people feel ashamed to ask God for help, especially if they haven't felt close to

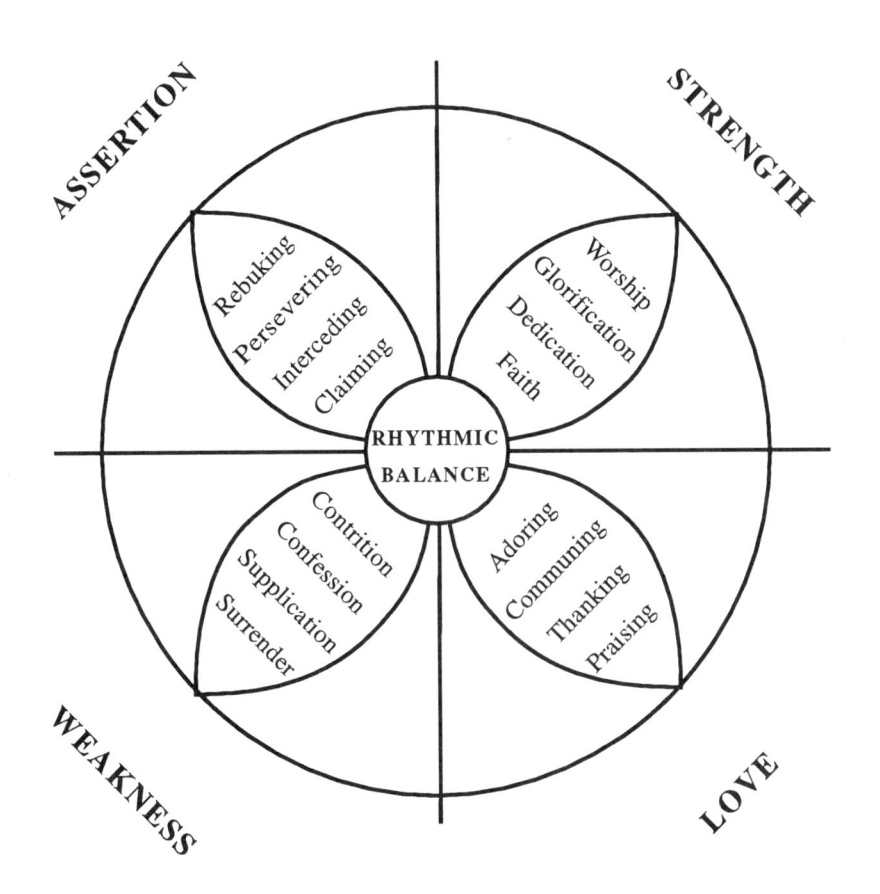

THE PRAYER COMPASS

ASSERTION
- Rebuking
- Persevering
- Interceding
- Claiming

STRENGTH
- Worship
- Glorification
- Dedication
- Faith

RHYTHMIC BALANCE

WEAKNESS
- Contrition
- Confession
- Supplication
- Surrender

LOVE
- Adoring
- Communing
- Thanking
- Praising

him before a crisis strikes. They don't realize that God's very nature offers mercy and grace to those who are suffering. A woman named Jaylene began her prayer life on the weakness pole.

Grace is God to the rescue.

She writes:

I'd been raised in a liturgical church, but in my university years I felt too sophisticated to even believe in a personal God. The universe ran on orderly principles which didn't need sentimental explanations such as the involvement of God. There was a ten year period when I don't think I uttered a single prayer.

It wasn't until my late thirties that I began to understand that a real friendship with God was even possible. I entered therapy with Dr. Montgomery and he talked openly about his friendship with Jesus. I felt angry. He insulted my intelligence by talking about a personal relationship with Divinity. But I had to admit that he was getting good results in healing the wounds in my personal life. He wasn't a kook. This made me consider what he was saying about God.

To be honest, I was envious. I wanted that for me. I wondered why God would talk to him and not to everybody around the world. Or maybe I just wasn't listening. The bottom line was that I had no idea how to reach God personally and was too embarrassed to ask for help.

Then a crisis crashed into my life. My fifteen year old daughter had a car accident and almost died in the emergency room. I got on my knees in the corridor and prayed for about an hour. A presence came over me that shifted me into another dimension of reality. I felt a peace, a clarity and an electricity. I continued praying, but now with every part of me.

The peace which descended on me that night has never left. I think that crisis cracked my shell. It drew out a greater love for my daughter than I had ever known. I felt willing to die for her. But it also helped me realize that God has that same love for me. I smiled later on that week when God seemed to whisper that I had been a hard nut to crack.

Weakness brings reliance on God. Grace is God to the rescue. This doesn't mean we should get stuck in a personality pattern of being helpless—pining and whining. It means that when life takes a turn for the worse, when the bottom seems to fall out, we simply pray, "Lord, help me in my weakness. Enter my situation and turn it around for good." Or we can exclaim as Peter did when he walked on water with the Lord and suddenly started sinking, "Help!"

Jesus felt a devastating weakness in the garden of Gethsemane. Face to face with capture, torture, humiliation and a terrifying death on the cross, he fell to the ground trembling and sweating drops of blood. He said, "Abba, Father, all things are possible to you; remove this cup from me; yet not what I will, but what you will" (Mk 14:36).

While in the throes of a season of weakness or dark night of the soul, we don't have to pretend we're up when we're really down. At the age of fourty-four, I experienced a mid-life crisis that hit me like a ninety-foot tidal wave. Within a four month period, I lost my home, business and health. All I had left was weakness. I visited Abbot David at the Pecos Benedictine Monastery for an hour of counseling. He wept with me as I told him of my sorrows.

He said, "Dan, God sometimes uses our weakness to dig a very big hole in the center of our beings. Then he fills this empty hole with his love." He mentioned two scriptures which really helped me. "[We have] won strength out of weakness" (Heb 11:34).

"Weeping may tarry for the night, but joy comes with the morning" (Ps 3:5). I left our meeting heartened. It took the entire next year for Abbot David's counsel to come true, but in that time I recovered completely and came to know the depth of God's love as never before.

In weakness, we feel contrite and humble. We confess our anxieties and pain. We make supplication for eventual strength. We rely on God for consolation.

Praying from Love

When one human being loves God for God's own sake, feels gratitude for all Jesus has done, or gives thanks for the comfort of the Holy Spirit, all heaven must burst into song. Christianity is all about love. "Love God with all your heart, mind, body and strength," said Jesus. "They will know you are my followers by your love." The expressions of prayer from the love pole include adoration, communion, thanksgiving and praise. The Psalmist notes that God inhabits the praise of His people (cf. Ps 22:3).

Our prayers from the love pole flow from our friendship and affection toward the Lord. A Carmelite lay brother named Brother Lawrence worked out an easy method for "prayer of the heart." While washing dishes in a monastic kitchen, and in whatever he did, he tried to maintain a "sweet and loving gaze toward God." A simple person, he fell head over heels in love with God and let that infuse everything, even to turning his "little omelet in the pan for God."[35]

Years ago I attended a weekly prayer meeting with a sister who was a hospital administrator. Sister Zita Marie radiated the love of God. She told me that she often prayed to be a channel for God's love, and asked this especially during the Mass and prayer meetings. It showed. Sister Zita had an incredible capacity to receive love from Christ and pour it out on others. Many times I would see her downtown giving hugs to homeless people or slipping her last couple of dollars to them. One day we were going to a restaurant for lunch together. Outside stood a man who hadn't bathed or shaved for days.

"Thank God for you, sir," exclaimed Sister Zita, shaking his hand. "Come in with us and I'll buy you lunch." The man smiled, joined us and wolfed his food as she asked him all about his life. He left looking like a new man. "God be praised we could sit with such a fine gentleman," she told me.

The week after Christmas of the same year, I met Sister Zita at our weekly prayer meeting. I figured she had flown back to her home state to visit her parents, but I was wrong. "Oh Dan," she said. "I had the most marvelous Christmas! At the village clinic where I work on Saturdays there is a little girl who contracted bone cancer of the leg. The doctors amputated her leg and said she would only live a couple more years. She took it so bravely! From her bedside she looked me in the eye and said, 'Sister Zita, will you please spend Christmas with my family?' I did so and it was the most blessed Christmas I've ever known."

One day my curiosity got the best of me and I asked Sister Zita how long she had been praying to be a channel of God's love. She smiled and then replied, "Thirty years."

Praying from Strength

Through strength we approach God in admiration for who he is and how he guides and blesses us. We feel confident in the Lord, knowing that he delights in us and that he has an inspired destiny for every one of us. The author of the letter to the Hebrews wrote: "Let us then with confidence draw near to the throne of grace, that we may receive mercy and find grace to help in time of need" (Heb 4:16).

In strength, we exult God for his goodness and mercy, we glorify Christ for shedding his blood for our sins, we express confidence in God's guidance for our lives and we joyfully worship the one true and living God.

As a psychology professor in a Catholic graduate school, I often engaged in live therapy demonstrations with student volunteers in order to show how counseling works. A woman named Mary volunteered for one of these sessions. Twenty-five students arranged their chairs into a circle around us. By the time we finished the hour session, many of them were openly weeping. I, too, had been moved to tears.

Mary's four year old niece Michelle suffered from a terminal illness. She was expected to die within the month. Mary showed me a picture of this little girl with an irresistible smile. "It isn't fair!" she grieved with pain and anger. "Michelle is so innocent. She loves her parents and she loves life. What can we possibly tell her? How can we talk to her about how God loves her when he's allowing her to die?"

"Mary, the highest priority is to walk this precious little girl across the bridge that represents the passage from death to eternal life in Christ. The family can work through their grief after she is gone. But right now Michelle needs your strength. She needs someone to hold her hand until Jesus welcomes her home."

"How can I do that, Dr. Montgomery? I feel terrified every night when I think about her situation. My stomach hurts so much that I can hardly eat. My sister and brother-in-law can't even talk about her death. None of us know what to tell her."

"Mary," I said, "maybe you are the one who can be a bridge from this life to the next for Michelle. She needs to understand that her death is not final and destructive. She needs to know that God's love will prevail and that great joy lies ahead. She is sick now but will be whole then. She is suffering now, but will be completely restored soon. I believe you can offer her emotional and spiritual support to prepare for her personal resurrection."

"But how can I explain this to her? She won't understand the concept of a resurrection."

"May I pray for you to feel new strength? Then your own calmness will assure her."

"Yes," Mary said, bowing her head.

I put my hand on her shoulder. "Father, infuse Mary with strength and confidence about the resurrection of the body and your great love of Michelle. We dedicate Michelle's life to the glory of Christ. Give Mary the power to help this little girl come to you."

Mary returned the following week noticeably strengthened. We positioned the desks around the room for a second session.

"It's working," Mary said. "I was able to comfort my sister and brother-in-law all week. I talked to Michelle about Jesus. She wants to meet him. But she asked why she has to die. I said that Jesus would tell her on the other side of the bridge to heaven."

"How did Michelle react?" I asked.

"She accepted it. She was very curious. When we finished talking, she wanted to eat lunch, and then play dolls. She smiled all week. I wish she didn't have to die!"

"Mary, you're building a wonderful bridge to Michelle's resurrection with the strength God is giving you. You're not alone. Jesus is with you, and so are we."

The following week Mary missed class to attend Michelle's funeral. When she returned a week later I expected her to be down, but she wasn't. I asked for an update.

Mary stepped to the front of the class and spoke with warmth and confidence. "I was with Michelle Wednesday evening when she died," she said. "She asked me to tell her again about the bridge where Jesus would take her hand. I held one hand and pretended we were walking across the bridge together. Her parents held her other hand. They didn't want to say good-bye out loud. The last thing Michelle said was, 'There's a light!...' and then her hands went limp."

Mary had received the gift of strength in a situation which demanded it. In the moment of Michelle's death, love surrounded the whole family and eternal life prevailed. In the afterglow, Mary seemed practically radiant with the glory of God. This woman had glimpsed the unseen realities beyond death, and Jesus began to restore all of them—Mary, Michelle and her parents—even during their loss. Mary was able to comfort others through her inspired strength and faith.

Praying from Assertion

Through assertion we approach God with determination and boldness. In a parable, Christ commended the assertive widow who kept badgering the judge until he gave her a fair ruling. God is always happy to hear from us. The assertion compass point teaches us to pray with power, laying our petitions before the Lord, interceding for others, resisting the evil one and claiming the promises of God.

In assertion, we prevail against evil in the Lord's name. We stand up for our values and confront those who would manipulate us. We pray courageously for the healing of hearts and bodies, for the grace to resist temptation, and for the gifts of the Holy Spirit to imbue us with power from on high.

My daughter Kimberly and I prayed assertively when she faced a crisis in the seventh grade. A classmate had physically attacked Kim. That night at home, we offered intercessory prayer for God to help her classmate; then we petitioned the Lord that the two of them would eventually become friends. Here's what happened in Kim's own words:

> I started junior high this year in a new state. It was hard to move from my home state and to leave all my friends. But my dad and mom moved and suddenly I was here. I really missed my old friends, but I made new friends in the first weeks of school and we hung out together.
>
> It turned out to be a pretty good semester. On the day grades came out I stood in line at the teacher's desk to get mine. When I looked at my grade card I couldn't believe it: straight A's. It was the first time in my life. I was so happy. But someone in the room didn't like my excitement.

The Prayer Compass / 159

Pearl had moved from another state this year, too. Only she hated it here. With a reputation for being tough and a good fighter, this girl seemed to hate junior high. When I shouted that I got a four point grade average, Pearl suddenly hated me. WHAM! She hit me several times before I even knew what happened. I hit her in the stomach to protect myself. Then she pulled my hair as hard as she could and I pulled hers.

After school I was in tears. I felt very disturbed. I didn't even want to go back to school the next day because Pearl had threatened me. I told my dad about it. He said that he would talk with the principal the next day. I didn't want him to do that because Pearl would say I ratted on her.

Later that night, Dad came into my room and said that we should pray about this. I didn't know what to say to God, so I just agreed with his prayer. Daddy asked God to help Pearl feel better about herself and about moving to New Mexico. He asked God that if it were possible, could he help Pearl and me become good friends instead of enemies. I opened my eyes and thought, *can God really do that?* I hoped it would come true!

The next day I was called to the principal's office. It was scary to face Pearl, her mother, my dad and the principal. Pearl and I had to talk about what happened and how we felt about each other. She said she didn't like me. I said I didn't like her. It didn't look too good.

For the next couple of weeks Pearl and I avoided each other. She told her friends that she was going to come after me, but she never did. Then the strangest thing happened. The next semester started and we got put in art class together. We ended up sitting together for two semesters. We had time to get to know each other.

As it turned out we have many things in common. We both moved to a new state last year and went through the same stress. We like the same music and enjoy laughing and joking.

A turning point came when Pearl's best friend Liz invited me to a movie with them. That weekend we went to the movies and had a fun time. Was God answering my prayers? It seemed like he was creating ways for Pearl and me to become good friends.

Now that the school year is over, Pearl and I do many things together. The anger between us has been turned into trust. I am looking forward to school next year. Pearl became a loyal friend.

Through this crisis I learned how to pray for something that seemed impossible. I discovered that God really can change enemies into friends, even if it takes a year to do it!

Prayer Is a Two Way Conversation

Sometimes the Spirit of Christ prays assertively through us, preparing us for challenges which lie ahead, although the challenges seem impossible at the time. One night three years ago I trekked down the stairs at midnight to make a peanut butter sandwich.

I had taken one bite and swallowed some milk, when the Holy Spirit began to flow through me. I thought it was a strange time and place for a spiritual experience. I began to pray in my prayer language, but this quickly shifted into singing in the Spirit. The Holy Spirit so infused my body that I began to dance for joy.

My body felt dazzled by God's love. Abruptly, I came to a halt. As though by an invisible hand, my body was turned north, east, south and west in rapid succession. My hands cupped themselves into the shape of a globe, which seemed to symbolize the earth. Suddenly I was inspired to speak in English. These words poured out of me, "I've called you to teach people about their personalities; to help them open their hearts to me. Through writing and speaking, I'll send the words I give you throughout the world." My body glowed with comfort as the visitation ended. I staggered back upstairs, wondering how a little known writer's words could span the globe.

Now, three years later, 30 million readers have come to read my magazine articles about how God works within our personalities. One article has appeared in 160 countries. I'm receiving letters from Japan, Indonesia, Europe, China, Australia and India. This year my book *The Manipulators*[36] (co-authored with Dr. Everett Shostrom) came out in Chinese and French translations. On the CBS Evening News, Dan Rather mentioned a more recent book—*How to Survive Practically Anything*.[37] Shortly afterward, I received a personal letter from the President of the United States, saying he had enjoyed the book. Jesus certainly knew what he was talking about when his Spirit prayed through me at midnight in my kitchen!

Mother Teresa writes: "What is essential is not what we say but what God tells us and what he tells others through us. Jesus always waits for us in silence. In silence he listens to us; in silence he speaks to our souls. In silence we are granted the privilege of listening to his voice."[38]

Thirteen

Change in Your Own Backyard

Danny Charles' mother stood a mere five feet tall, yet to him she seemed like a Goliath. Ever since he could remember, she was pushing him forward into the world of people, regardless of how shy and introverted he felt.

He recalled a scene from childhood.

Mother dragged me by the wrist downtown to the shoe store. I was about ten years old. "Mr. Hoffman," she told the owner of the store in a high pitched voice, "get five pairs of shoes out here right this minute. Danny needs a new pair for his birthday party. Do you have any colors other than black? Black is so dull!"

Mr. Hoffman hopped like a rabbit back and forth, opening so many shoeboxes it looked like Christmas. Wrapping paper and empty boxes were everywhere. Other people came into the store, but they had to wait. "There's the perfect pair," she exclaimed, pointing to a red pair of tie-up shoes. I cringed. I'd be the laughingstock of my school. My stomach swirled.

"Don't you just love them?" she asked without waiting for my reply. "Wrap them up in nice paper, Mr. Hoffman. Danny loves them!"

This forty-year-old man vividly remembered many such episodes. He shared another story, this time about his teenage years:

> Mother made me join a young men's organization called DeMolays. I was bored to death and hated the weekly meetings. I pleaded with my father to help me, to tell my mother that I didn't have to go. But she got furious anytime either of us would mention the possibility of quitting. "Danny Charles, you are a not-nice boy. I just bought you some new shirts for school. How dare you say you want to quit DeMolays!" Dad would roll his eyes back and hide behind his newspaper.
>
> Around seventeen I started protesting more strongly. So did she. She'd scream, grimace and come barging into my bedroom yelling that I had no right to disagree with her about anything. When I finally became Master Counselor of the DeMolays chapter at the age of eighteen, she arranged for pictures in the local newspaper and a large reception held at the Masonic Lodge. My face was red as a beet the whole time but my mother never noticed.
>
> It wasn't just DeMolays. I felt invaded daily, my dignity tromped upon and my feelings disparaged. My chest often felt numb with tension and my stomach cramped with unexpressed anger. Anger was not allowed in our home, unless it was Mother's anger. She didn't get angry just at home. The older I got, the more I noticed that Mom was loud, aggressive and outspoken everywhere, except when she wanted to make a good impression. Then she'd instantly change, becoming all smiles, sweetness and charm. Yet no one dared mention her anxiety and driving need to control everyone, especially me.

Danny Charles' mother handled his adult life with the same antagonism and smothering nosiness. She opposed his vocation, took a strong stand against his marriage and contradicted whatever he believed in. In his thirties, he thought, *I don't know who I am. My mother dominates my thoughts, feelings and actions. God help me!*

Danny Charles learned in psychotherapy about the compass of the self and applied it vigorously to heal his personality. He took growth stretches into assertion and strength to find the courage to cut the psychological umbilical cord to his mother. He wanted Christ to be the center of his life.

He flourished in his new growth, experiencing the joy of intimacy, identity and community with others. Danny Charles finally made his declaration of independence from his mother. He rooted out her moodiness, criticisms and negativity from his core. For the first time, he lived life with freedom and joy, trusting the Divine Spirit of Christ to guide him daily.

Then the strangest thing happened. He felt God calling him to return to his mother and help her. "No way!" he said to the still, small voice. "I can't stand to have anything to do with Mom ever again!" But over months the gentle voice prevailed. "Danny," the voice explained, "I've set you free to be your real self. You've learned how to stand on your own feet, handle vulnerability, express yourself and love others. Now it's time to love your mother."

Reluctantly, Danny Charles made arrangements to spend several months living with his mother. She was now eighty-years-old, and her contrary ways had put off her other children and grandchildren. Her husband had died. She lived alone.

Their first months together were stormy. His mother wasn't about to hear from her son what she had avoided hearing for a lifetime. He'd try to delicately bring into her awareness how her aggression burned bridges to people, or how her constant criticisms drove people away. She exploded into tirades that lasted for hours.

The fourth month Danny Charles had a reckoning with God. "Dear Lord, you sent me here to help Mom, but she's only getting worse. I'm going crazy. I'll stay one more week and then I'm leaving until she dies."

A few days later Danny Charles and his mother took a trip together to a town sixty miles away. In the middle of the drive, the inner voice of the Lord prompted Danny Charles to go for broke. He took a breath and started speaking softly, but firmly, "Mom, I've got to say a few things and I'd appreciate it if you'd just listen." He saw her set her jaw, stiffen her neck and glare straight ahead. "You were raised as a child piano prodigy and had your own radio show by the age of twelve. They called you 'Queen of the Air.'

"By thirteen you played for two civic clubs in town. You were the most colorful and talented of your ten brothers and sisters. Your mother thought you walked on water. Everybody thought you were the center of the universe—including you. All your childhood confidence turned you into a sassy know-it-all. As an adult and a parent you believed that the world was at your command.

"To get your way you threw temper tantrums, screamed a lot, made ugly faces and harangued for hours. But to the townspeople you put on smiles and played the piano with a passion. I've been trying to have a two-way conversation with you my whole life, but it's been impossible. You butt in, jump to conclusions, get defensive, become nervous and do everything in your power to keep from hearing the truth about your own behavior.

"I just want to say there's a better way. For whatever years you have left, you can choose to become a positive, sensitive and caring woman who uses humor and affection instead of aggression and hostility. I love you, but I know that if you don't change soon, you'll die without ever having had a single decent conversation with your own son."

His mother sat in silence for the next ten minutes. She looked white as a sheet, her arms folded over her chest, and her neck slightly bowed. Then she spoke in a quiet voice. "Danny Charles, every word you've said is true. I've never understood my life until just now. God has spoken to me through you."

Over the next two weeks, Anna changed so noticeably that all the family members could talk of little else. She showed some humility now, shared the limelight with others and listened while others spoke. Her old arrogance shifted into quiet confidence, like one who has lived fully but can learn from others as well. Her aggression all but disappeared. Instead, she demonstrated good cheer bringing good cheer and a wonderful ability to build people up. Her self-absorption was transformed into tender caring. Whether through phone calls or thoughtful cards or in person at family get-togethers, Anna could be counted on to say a hearty "I love you and may the Lord bless you!"

The story of Danny Charles and his mother Anna shows how anyone can change, even in fundamental ways, as long as they live. By accepting God's grace and applying the principles of the personality compass, people can find their way home to intimacy, identity and community—right in their own backyard.

I know. I'm Danny Charles.

A WORD TO THE READER

I am an author who enjoys hearing from my readers. Writing is a lonely profession. I stare into the computer monitor for hundreds of hours, longing to see the facial reactions of those to whom I'm writing. Sometimes I wonder whether I'm making any contact at all, especially on the emotional level.

That's why I am so thrilled when people write and tell me how they felt about certain stories or passages, or how they responded when I disclosed my own struggles or triumphs. A dialogue between me and readers brings me great joy. I would love to hear how you have applied the principles in this book to your own life, and what has been the result. If you send me a photo, I'll tack it onto my bulletin board.

If you are a priest, religious or counselor and would like to know about my other books dealing with the compass of the self or Compass Therapy, please drop me a line. If you would like me to speak at a national conference, retreat or church seminar, please write and I'll send you a résumé and list of workshops and speaking topics. If you would like to begin a group book study in a church or mental health setting, turn the page and read the guidelines for doing so.

For now, thank you for reading *God and Your Personality*. I hope it has enriched your life.

Dr. Dan Montgomery
c/o Pauline Books & Media
50 St. Paul's Avenue,
Boston, MA 02130

HOW TO START A "GOD AND YOUR PERSONALITY" BOOK STUDY

Dear Leader,

Here are 12 suggestions for starting a *God and Your Personality* book study in your neighborhood, parish or home prayer meeting.

1. To develop people's interest, have your local Christian bookstore stock books for interested friends, acquaintances and church members. Also, anyone can directly order the book by calling Pauline Books & Media at 1-800-876-4463.
2. Tell people that you are interested in facilitating a *God and Your Personality* book study that will begin as soon as you have three or more members. List names and phone numbers of those interested. If you are already in an existing class or prayer group, suggest that the focus might be on a book study process for several months.
3. Set a starting date and an overall time-frame. I suggest one hour per week for 12-15 weeks.
4. Start each meeting with at least five minutes of prayer time. Let people pray silently or out loud for the presence of Christ to guide the group's progress.
5. The book study is carried on in a round-robin fashion. Each person reads three or so paragraphs, then shares his or her experience, need and hope. As the group leader, you are but a trusted servant, not a dictator or monopolizer. Simply let people share (you may need to set an agreed upon time limit of 3-5 minutes). Then invite the next reader to begin. If a person reads and does not wish to express a personal comment, he or she is free to do so.

6. Let members know there is no cross-talk, judgment or advice-giving. Individuals are free to express personal experiences *about their own lives,* but must withhold comments about others. Stress the need for confidentiality, which is the life blood of self-disclosure and trust.
7. *Trust the group process and the presence of the Holy Spirit to draw people out and help them to be healed.* Develop a warm interpersonal climate free from moralizing.
8. Anything human is worthy of understanding. God accepts us as we are and desires us to become more real. People are healed and encouraged when they confide from the heart—"confess your sins to one another, and pray for one another, that you may be healed" (Jas 5:16). If a member tells another member what they should or should not do, jump in with a gentle reminder that there should be no cross-talk, judgment, or advice-giving.
9. With ten minutes remaining, announce that only one or two more people can read or share. With five minutes left, ask everyone to mark the stopping point in their books. Stand up. Join hands. Invite someone to lead the Lord's Prayer.
10. Dismiss the group on time. Allow people to mill around.
11. When the book study has been completed, take a vote to see if the group wishes to begin a new cycle at the beginning of the book. If so, let a new volunteer take over the servant/leader role. Pass these guidelines to the new volunteer.
12. *God and Your Personality Groups* can be open-ended and run year-round. Newcomers can join the group at anytime and continue as long as they wish. The only criteria for membership is the desire to experience God at work within your personality.

God bless you and stay in touch,
Dan Montgomery, Ph.D.

Notes

One
God and Your Personality

1. Ignace Lepp, *The Depths of the Soul* (Staten Island, NY: Alba House, 1965), p. 39.

Two
Compass of the Self

2. Henri Nouwen, *Reaching Out: The Three Movements of the Spiritual Life* (New York: Doubleday, 1975), p. 12.

3. Frederick Copleston, *Contemporary Philosophy* (New York: Newman Press, 1966), p. 107.

4. Bernadette Vetter, *My Journey, My Prayer* (New York: William W. Sadlier, 1977), p. 18.

Three
The Core of Personality

5. Richard McBrien, *Catholicism* (San Francisco: Harper Collins, 1981), pp. 1134-1135.

6. Adrian van Kaam, *The Woman At the Well* (New Jersey: Dimension Books, 1976), p. 146.

Four
The Dependent Christian

7. Richard McBrien, *Catholicism* (San Francisco: Harper Collins, 1981), p. 990.

8. Adrian van Kaam, *Religion and Personality* (Englewood Cliffs, NJ: Prentice-Hall, 1964), p. 154-55.

9. Adrian van Kaam, *Spirituality and the Gentle Life* (New Jersey: Dimension Books, 1974), p. 97.

Five
The Aggressive Christian

10. Adrian van Kaam, *Religion and Personality* (Englewood Cliffs, NJ, 1964), p. 157.

11. Karen Horney, *Our Inner Conflicts* (New York: W. W. Norton, 1945), p. 203.

12. Keith Miller, *Please Love Me* (Waco, TX: Word Books, 1977), p. 66.

13. Rollo May, *The Art of Counseling* (New York: W.W. Norton, 1977), p. 224.

Six
The Withdrawn Christian

14. Paul Tournier, *The Strong And The Weak* (Philadelphia: Westminster Press, 1963).

15. Adrian van Kaam, *Religion and Personality* (Englewood Cliffs, NJ: Prentice-Hall, 1964), p. 156.

16. Anthony de Mello, *Song of the Bird* (New York: Image, 1992), p. 32.

Seven
The Controlling Christian

17. John Powell, *The Christian Vision* (Allen, TX: Tabor Publishing, 1984), p. 54.

Eight
Beyond Manipulation

18. John Powell, *The Christian Vision* (Allen, TX: Tabor Pub., 1984), p. 12.

Nine

Techniques for Transformation

20. Thomas Merton, *The Seven Storey Mountain* (New York: Harcourt, Brace and Co., 1948), p. 381.

21. Eugene Peterson, *The Message* (Colorado Springs, CO: NavPress, 1993), p. 31.

22. Dan Montgomery, *How to Survive Practically Anything* (Ann Arbor, MI: Servant Publications, 1993), pp. 143-150.

23. Roberto Assagioli, *Psychosynthesis* (New York: Viking, 1965), pp. 214-215.

Ten

Befriending Your Unconscious

24. Cardinal Leo Suenens, *A New Pentecost?* (New York: Seabury Press, 1974), p. xiii.

25. Richard McBrien, *Catholicism* (San Francisco: Harper Collins, 1981), p. 1089.

26. Martin Marty, "Something Real and Lumpy," *U.S. Catholic,* vol. 44, May 1979, p. 24.

27. Joseph Goldbrunner, *Holiness is Wholeness and Other Essays* (Notre Dame, IN: University of Notre Dame Press, 1964), p. 14.

28. Thomas Merton, *No Man Is An Island* (New York: Harcourt, Brace and Co., 1983), p. 126.

29. Cardinal Suenens, *A New Pentecost?* (New York: Seabury Press, 1974), p. 103.

Eleven

Images of God

30. Albert Haase, *Swimming in the Sun* (Cincinnati, OH: St. Anthony Messenger Press, 1993), p. 7.

31. Richard McBrien, *Catholicism* (San Francisco: Harper Collins, 1981), p. 333.

32. Vatican Council II. "The Church in the Modern World" *(Gaudium et spes). The Documents of Vatican II.* Ed. Walter M. Abbott. (New York: America Press, 1966), pp. 199-308.

33. Adrian van Kaam, *Religion and Personality* (Englewood Cliffs, NJ: Prentice-Hall, 1964), p. 158.

Twelve

The Prayer Compass

34. Richard McBrien, *Catholicism* (San Francisco: Harper Collins, 1981), p. 332.

35. Brother Lawrence, *Practicing the Presence of God* (Beaumont, TX: The Seed Sowers, 1973), p. 43.

36. Everett Shostrom and Dan Montgomery, *The Manipulators* (Nashville: Abingdon Press, 1990).

37. Dan Montgomery, *How to Survive Practically Anything* (Ann Arbor, MI: Servant, 1993).

38. Mother Teresa, *Heart of Joy* (Ann Arbor, MI: Servant, 1987), p. 93.

Index

A
agape 142
anger 50, 114
art box 106
artesian well 35
assertion 24, 51, 134

B
balanced personality 21, 92, 100

C
compass of the self 19, 167
Compass Therapy 167
core 38
courage
   of imperfection 104
   of perseverence 71
   to grow 39
   to love 96

D
defensiveness 96, 105
depression 113, 125, 127

E
effortless effort 105
evil 118

G
grace 109, 153
growth 39, 111
guilt 109

I
interior life 133

J
joy 64, 74, 111, 133, 160

L
"LAWS" 22, 96
love 23, 64, 134

M
masochism 24

P
partial personality style 28
perspective
   partial 23, 29
   dependent 44, 138
   aggressive 56, 140
   withdrawn 70, 140
   controlling 80, 141
Pharisees 20, 25
play 142
prayer 149

R
rhythm 112
rigidity 39

S
sin 39, 106
strength 27, 134

V
virtue
   of caring 100
   of courage 100
   of esteem 100
   of humility 100

W
weakness 25, 134

St. Paul Book & Media Centers

ALASKA
750 West 5th Ave., Anchorage, AK 99501; 907-272-8183

CALIFORNIA
3908 Sepulveda Blvd., Culver City, CA 90230; 310-397-8676
5945 Balboa Ave., San Diego, CA 92111; 619-565-9181
46 Geary Street, San Francisco, CA 94108; 415-781-5180

FLORIDA
145 S.W. 107th Ave., Miami, FL 33174; 305-559-6715

HAWAII
1143 Bishop Street, Honolulu, HI 96813; 808-521-2731

ILLINOIS
172 North Michigan Ave., Chicago, IL 60601; 312-346-4228

LOUISIANA
4403 Veterans Memorial Blvd., Metairie, LA 70006; 504-887-7631

MASSACHUSETTS
50 St. Paul's Ave., Jamaica Plain, Boston, MA 02130; 617-522-8911
Rte. 1, 885 Providence Hwy., Dedham, MA 02026; 617-326-5385

MISSOURI
9804 Watson Rd., St. Louis, MO 63126; 314-965-3512

NEW JERSEY
561 U.S. Route 1, Wick Plaza, Edison, NJ 08817; 908-572-1200

NEW YORK
150 East 52nd Street, New York, NY 10022; 212-754-1110
78 Fort Place, Staten Island, NY 10301; 718-447-5071

OHIO
2105 Ontario Street, Cleveland, OH 44115; 216-621-9427

PENNSYLVANIA
510 Holstein Street, Bridgeport, PA 19405; 610-277-7728

SOUTH CAROLINA
243 King Street, Charleston, SC 29401; 803-577-0175

TENNESSEE
4811 Poplar Ave., Memphis, TN 38117; 901-761-2987

TEXAS
114 Main Plaza, San Antonio, TX 78205; 210-224-8101

VIRGINIA
1025 King Street, Alexandria, VA 22314; 703-549-3806

GUAM
285 Farenholt Ave., Suite 308, Tamuning, Guam 96911; 671-649-4377

CANADA
3022 Dufferin Street, Toronto, Ontario, Canada M6B 3T5; 416-781-9131